THE BALACHITES and THE STRANGE CASE OF MARTIN RICHTER

These two plays give an admirable indication of the breadth
of Eveling's vision and the variety of his stylistic talent.
Both plays follow the development of a certain idea with an
intriguing combination of logic and absurdity which
characterizes his work.

THE BALACHITES is set in an empty house, where three
characters, a retired gardener, a super-annuated scientist
and a veteran corporal, discuss their differences in attitude
to the value of life. It is not until a young couple come to
look at the house that we realise that the original trio are
ghosts, not strictly speaking malevolent, but ghosts all the
same. At first the natural and supernatural maintain their
distance from one another, but gradually the two worlds join
forces in an attempt to re-create the innocence of Eden, an
attempt which must fail.

THE STRANGE CASE OF MARTIN RICHTER follows the
political rise and fall of a potential dictator, who turns out to
be no more than a butler in the house of a wealthy industrial-
ist. Parallels with the rise of fascism are unmistakeable -
the play is set in Germany, where a racial minority, the
Swebians, are persecuted for no other reason than that they
are Swebians, the rising party is called the National Health
Party - but beyond these similarities, the play can be seen
as a political parable based on the precept that 'To him that
has shall be given. To him that has not even that which he
has shall be taken away.'

Stanley Eveling was born in 1925 in Newcastle upon Tyne.
After three years in the Army, he read English and
Philosophy at Newcastle and took a further degree in
Philosophy at Oxford. He now teaches Philosophy at
Edinburgh University. Stanley Eveling has written several
plays for stage, radio and television and was recently
awarded the Scottish Television Award for the best playwright of 1968, the first year in which this annual prize was
presented. Stanley Eveling is the most discussed Scottish
playwright to emerge during the sixties, a moralist with a
natural flair for putting the problems and dilemmas of
modern life onto the stage.

PLAYSCRIPT 20

'the balachites' & 'the strange case of martin richter'

stanley eveling

CALDER AND BOYARS · LONDON

First published in Great Britain 1970
by Calder and Boyars Limited
18 Brewer Street London W 1

SBN 7145 0100 X Cloth edition
SBN 7145 0101 8 Paper edition

Printed in Great Britain
by The Pitman Press,
Bath, Somerset

CONTENTS

THE BALACHITES

THE BALACHITES was first performed on 30 July 1963 at the Traverse Theatre, Edinburgh. The play was produced by Terry Lane with the following cast:

ALBERT	Ian Trigger
BENJAMIN	Tony Healey
CORPORAL	Richard Gill
GEORGE	Keith Taylor
MIRIAM	Rosamund Dickson

ACT ONE

(ALBERT, an old man, is lying on a couch in the
centre of the stage. On the floor there is a grey carpet
almost as ancient as himself. At stage right there is a
large mirror on a stand and at stage left a door with
paint peeling. There is a window at the back of the
stage but it is covered over with boards. At each side
of the window and widely spaced from it there is a
balachite but the large central balachite is concealed by
the sofa. These balachites must become illuminated
during certain moments in the action, as will be seen,
but otherwise they are to look like the dull stones they
really are. To the left of the door there is a large,
battered trunk.

When the scene opens ALBERT is looking at one of the
balachites. He fingers it, chuckles to himself and then
sighs. He wanders irresolutely about behind the sofa,
sighs and then lies down on the sofa. He is wearing his
hat. His dress must be stained and old and as if he were,
most probably, a retired gardener. He is smoking a
pipe. He settles himself, blows clouds of smoke out of
his mouth, coughs, spits, clears his throat noisily and
spits again. Then he draws hard on his pipe and begins
to puff out signals.)

ALBERT. Is there anybody there? Is there anybody? One
puff for yes, two puffs for no. (Pause) Silence, utter
and complete.

(He begins to sing quietly to himself)

'There's a great green moggy in the heavens,
There's a great green moggy in the sky,

There's a great green moggy in the heavens
And I'll go to that moggy when I die,

(More sadly)

And I'll go to that moggy when I die,

(Pause)

And I'll go to that moggy when I die. '

(Pause)

Mmmmm.

(Pause)

Hat says go. Pipe says go. Sofa says go. Shirt says go.
Body says go. Bloody walls say go. World says go. All
systems say GO.

(He grips the sofa. Begins to twist and shake.)

Wheeeeeeee.

(Pause)

Mmmmm.

(He puffs on his pipe again.)

Returned to life.

(He begins to sing quietly to himself again)

'I'm not very cheerful, I'm not very glad,
I haven't had the troubles that I ought to have had,
I've lived like a pig and I've slept all day,
And I've raged like a fiend when I didn't get my way,
Oh, dear me.

Moggy is white
In the moon, in the light,
His cry is heard

As he swallows a bird,
Oh, dear me.'

I've sung that song.

(Pause)

Yes. I've sung that song. Me, I'm always singing. Yes.
I am musical. In this little wild house my corncrake
song is heard. For whose ears? Mine. I am. What?
Tough as an old boot.

(He pinches himself.)

Yes. Dead as mutton. Dead. Stiff. Rigid. Eyes as
remote as stars. Thought at infinity. Can't get me. No.
Dead. Almost. Not quite. One foot in.

(He raises one leg.)

One out. Dead, done, finished. In me prime. For ever
and ever, amen.

(He grunts, groans, stretches, yawns, rises, faces the
audience, sniffs, blows his nose, gets stiffly down onto
his knees, puts his hands together.)

Let us pray.

(He remembers his hat. Takes it off.)

Hats off.

(He puts it back on again.)

Just for a change.

(Composes himself.)

Dear father and mother of old age, sickness and death;
visit me, an old, old, old man... such an old man...

(He sniffs, wipes his eyes.)

With plagues, boils and misery. Like you have done.
I've lived an evil life. Make me suffer, great things,
great, malevolent old so and so, older than me by a
long chalk, make me sad.

(Gets up.)

Rubbish. Talking to myself.

(He goes over to the looking glass. Stares at it, stares
into it. Smiles, simpers. Adopts a very loving, sickly
expression.)

Good morning, love. Good morning, darling. Ooh, it's
lovely. Little red mouths, all puckered up. Soft red
rosebuds, guzzling each other. I want to eat you.

(He raises his finger.)

Here's my finger; here's your finger. Touch.

(He puts his finger to the glass.)

Cool fingers. My flesh finger, your glass finger...
touch. Unpleasant.

(Pause)

Mirror ghost, smile. Mirror ghost, snarl.

(He bares his teeth and snarls into the mirror.)

Mirror ghost, come forth. Out of that room, please.
Talk to me, tell me what you think. Back when I go
back, forward when I go forward, mouth open when
mine is; not a bloody sound. Horrible. Voiceless
satirist. Say something yourself, will you? Be vastly
original. What?

(He opens his mouth and speaks a silent 'what' to the
glass.)

Of limited power. Just the same, noise or no noise. Do
a dance.

(He stares into the mirror. He peers intently into it. He whispers to it.)

I'm afraid of you, you dreadful, old bloodless, glass animal. You make me afraid. Who's hypnotising who?

(He speaks very slowly)

Breath... in. Breath... out. Breathe deeply, deeply, deeply... thing in the mirror. Sleep... sleep.

(He droops.)

Fast asleep. Now... dance.

(He does a slow, grotesque dance.)

Slowly. Slop, slop, hop, hop. Left foot, right foot.
Dance, dance, dance. It's dancing. Good. Mirror ghost, dance. Listen to the song.
'When I was a man and not a glass ghost
I didn't dance here until I was lost
But I am now in a screen of glass
And I look at a world that I cannot grasp,
Oh, dear me.'

(He stops dancing. Stares at the mirror, suddenly beats his fist against it.)

I don't love you, you horrible old image. Not, not, not.

(Pause)

Compose yourself.

(He goes back to the couch and lies down.)

BENJAMIN. (Heard coming upstairs) Albert! Albert! I'm coming for you, Albert. Do you hear, you old sod, I'm coming to get you, Albert?

ALBERT. Shhh.

(He puts his hat over his eyes and pretends to go to

sleep. BENJAMIN enters. He is dressed in faded pin stripe trousers and an old black coat. He should suggest a decayed city gentleman or a superannuated scientist.)

BENJAMIN. Where is the filthy old lump? Albert! Ah, there he is.

(He grabs ALBERT by the shoulder and shakes him.)

Wake up, you bloody old object. What are you sleeping in your hat for? Eh?

ALBERT. Art thou, fatal vision, as sensible to feeling as to sight? Are you? Well?

BENJAMIN. What are you doing, snottering on that couch?

ALBERT. Resting between labours. I have fasted long and prayed into the morning and now I fain would sleep.

BENJAMIN. You've been talking to your old wooden thing again, haven't you? You want to watch it, my lad. You want to watch it. It'll get you, alright. You see if it don't. It'll be after you. You'll wake up screaming one morning in some filthy old cell with no teeth and the wooden thing smiling down at you from the wall. All running with blood.

ALBERT. I will not. I am one of the saved. The wooden thing will one day stump into the room and say 'Arise, Albert, from thy couch, and push off.'

(BENJAMIN goes over to his basket, which he has brought in with him and begins to rummage in it. He hums to himself. ALBERT, having delivered himself of his last remark, sinks back onto the sofa but BENJAMIN's movements rouse him and he tries to see what he is doing.)

BENJAMIN.   'Cheese is delicious, cheese is nice,
            Cheese is the stuff for fat grey mice,
            Put it in a trap, they walk right in,
            Crack goes the trap and their spines cave in.

14

Blood, blood, blood.'

ALBERT. You horrible old beast. What have you got there? Eh? What have you got?

BENJAMIN. Nothing. I've got nothing. I ask you to believe that, Albert.

ALBERT. You have, you have. What have you got? Eh?

BENJAMIN. Nothing... nothing. I was... looking for something, that's all. Just looking to see if the something that I was looking for was there... in me basket... but it isn't.

ALBERT. What was it, then?

BENJAMIN. Eh? Oh, in the basket? Oh, nothing Albert. Nothing, really. It doesn't matter.

(Pause)

Oh, I remember.

ALBERT. Well, what was it that you remember that isn't anything and you were looking for in your bloody basket and it isn't there and it doesn't matter.

BENJAMIN. A present.

ALBERT. A present? What sort of present?

BENJAMIN. A plant, Albert. A little green plant. You've always been fond of plants, Albert.

ALBERT. I have?

BENJAMIN. Yes, you've always been fond of plants, Albert. That I do know. If ever I were to ask you what you would like, it's always been plants for as long as I can remember. Plants. Very peculiar. All kinds; long, thin tapering ones, with blue heads, whatever they are, and thick, fat, gross ones, full of juice, with great green leaves, like sponges; and red flowers, all drowsy

15

and nodding on the stalk; and bees buzzing. Very peculiar.

ALBERT. Plants are nice. What's so funny about that? I like plants. I always have and I always will. They are very pleasant things... What about my present?

BENJAMIN. It was a cactus.

ALBERT. Where is it, then?

BENJAMIN. I forgot, you see, Albert... what I forgot to buy you for a present was a cactus. It was in a shop... in the window. I saw it in the window... lovely green spines and purple leaves, Albert. It was in a brown pot ... very expensive. I remember saying 'I'll buy that for Albert.' I remember that thought crossed my mind. I nearly went in and bought it... but I forgot.

ALBERT. Liar. You couldn't forget.

BENJAMIN. I did, I did. I forgot. Just like that. One minute I was thinking, 'I'll buy that cactus for Albert' and the next minute I wasn't thinking anything of the kind.

ALBERT. You forgot deliberately. If you forgot... you forgot deliberately.

BENJAMIN. (Softly) Perhaps I did. Perhaps I did.

ALBERT. Benjamin.

BENJAMIN. Hmmm.

ALBERT. Benjamin! Listen to what I'm saying.

BENJAMIN. What, then?

ALBERT. Why, in God's name, do you not like plants, Benjamin?

BENJAMIN. In God's name, who said I didn't?

ALBERT. You didn't say you didn't... but you don't, do you?

BENJAMIN. How do you mean, like them?

ALBERT. Well, like I like them.

BENJAMIN. Like you like them I don't suppose I do. No, I don't suppose so. Anyway... how the hell can you like plants? It's ridiculous to like plants. Plants don't feel anything... they don't talk, do they? They are... just long and short, coloured, growing, dry, juicy... how the hell <u>can</u> I like plants?

ALBERT. They're funny things to like, certainly. But I like them.

BENJAMIN. Do you like rivers? Do you like rivers, and do you like rocks?

ALBERT. (Ruminatively) Rivers?

BENJAMIN. And rocks? And things like that? Do you like bloody dust particles? Floating about. Making lovely colours, refracting light. Do you like light?

ALBERT. You know I like rocks, Benjamin.

BENJAMIN. (With great indignation) Rocks! And rivers and shrubs and dust and light and shade, and atoms and molecules and mesons and protons and the average man and the typical housewife and the number seven and the square on the hypotenuse. You, Albert, like everything!

ALBERT. I don't like what I can't see, Benjamin.

BENJAMIN. Huh! You, Albert, are a phenomenon. Do you like people, Albert? What about that? Do you like <u>me</u>, Albert? What about me?

ALBERT. Live things. Things that wriggle and breathe. Well. I don't like people, Benjamin. Animals are impossible to like.

17

BENJAMIN. Then you are a cruel and horrible and twisted phenomenon, Albert. There is absolutely no doubt about that. So you don't like people, eh. It's people you don't like. It's me you don't like.

ALBERT. If I like plants, Benjamin, then I don't like people. People are more peculiar. Do you see that?

BENJAMIN. See what? There's nothing to see.

ALBERT. People... are... er, too adjacent... too near. Like myself. I'm too close to myself, Benjamin, you see, too adjacent... necessary. I like what is outside, away, far off, finished, created. I like things like that. People are too close, warm, hot, inside, not finished, open, possible, flushed... with things like... feelings, thoughts in feeling; they grope about, (Vehemently) animals;... they have eyes, lines, expressions... on their faces, things to be understood, mysteries, secrets... skeletons slumped in cupboards, veils, darkness in minds, corridors with dead thoughts drifting from window to window, sighing. Animals... in the day, walking from point to point; in the night... tied to their beds, thinking, twisting about.

(He begins to perform)

'I've told you and I won't tell you again. Now then. That's me last word. I've warned you. I'm telling you... I won't let him. He's got no right. He's awful... Where did it go? Who's got it? Where did I put it? Bugger off. (In mock consternation) It's under the bed. It's in the sheets. It's creeping about in the room. I've got... plague, pox, the creeping paralysis. I won't live the night. God.'

(He turns his attention back to BENJAMIN.)

What are you doing? What have you got in that basket, eh?

(While ALBERT is ruminating BENJAMIN has been rummaging in the basket which he brought in with him. On ALBERT's question he gets up, tossing all the stuff

18

back into the basket and walks over to the wall. He
sniffs and looks around carefully.)

BENJAMIN. You've been doing it again. You've been doing
it again, haven't you? How many times have I told you
not to do it... how many times... hundreds... and
you've been doing it again. I've reasoned with you, I've
pleaded with you, I have cajoled you. I have humbled
myself. All to no avail. You old nig nog. You're as soft
as butter. You just get up, quietly, without a qualm and
bloody well do it again.

ALBERT. I'm not listening, Benjamin. I can't hear a word
you say.

BENJAMIN. You've been stuffing them rodents with bread-
crumbs again, haven't you?

ALBERT. If you are referring to those tiny creatures who
inhabit the wainscot and who occasionally and shyly
sniff their way into our drawing room, if you are
adverting to our delicate, furry friends...

BENJAMIN. Mice, bloody mice, rodents, sharp teethed,
disease ridden scavengers.

ALBERT. Friends. (Airily) Well, yes, I did, as a matter
of fact, scatter a few dried crumbs inadvertently in the
area of their small burrow. I'm not ashamed, Benjamin,
I am not ashamed.

BENJAMIN. Then you are an idiot then. And it's just as
well I'm not as stupid as you or we'd all be dead in our
beds, I can tell you. But for my foresight, Albert, we'd
be stiff in our beds. Where's them traps?

ALBERT. Traps!

BENJAMIN. Traps. Listen, Albert, it can't go on, you see.
It can't be done. You see, Albert, you'd have all the
rabbits and bears and voles and lame ducks in creation
in one room and you'd be feeding them, and all the
bloody birds with cracked wings and weasels and
laughing jackasses with broken jaws and every little

bloody creepy crawler and all the bloody lot and it can't
be done. Do you see that?

ALBERT. There'll be no traps here, Benjamin. Let that be
understood.

BENJAMIN. (To himself) Be calm, then. Don't enrage
yourself. Don't let your temper get the better of yourself. Sit quietly for a minute and then the red haze'll
go. It will, Benjamin, it will.

ALBERT. There'll be no traps. No. No traps. No.

BENJAMIN. (Enraged) There are traps. There are
hundreds of traps. Traps with teeth, traps with trees
on them and ferns that elephants fall into and roar there
all night. There are traps with lovely food in them and
poison and there are traps with bloody goats in them
and men in trees waiting to bang their guns. There are
millions of traps, the bloody universe is littered with
traps and that, and that is exactly how it should be.
Traps, traps, traps.

(He snaps his teeth together.)

Got yer. Like that. Like you crack lice on your finger
nail. See.

ALBERT. (Gently) It's horrible though, Benjamin. Isn't
it, it's very nasty.

BENJAMIN. (More calmly. And sadly) Well... well...
just you sit quiet, Albert, now, and I'll tell you something. It's sad, this, what I have to tell you, Albert, but
never mind. Just you sit and listen.

ALBERT. I know about traps. I know about those things.
They have little wooden boards and they have a spring
in the middle and when the mouse nibbles the cheese
the spring cracks down and they squeak. I've heard
them. They give a long, high squeal or squeak and it's
horrible. The blood goes onto their teeth and they
squeak.

BENJAMIN. That's true. I know that. They squeak. And the blood does go onto their teeth. Mice have pink blood. Which is worse than human blood. It's not pleasant, Albert. But listen. That's not what you don't know about. That's only a little particular fact and it just makes you sad. You mustn't go by the feeling, Albert. (Getting indignant again) That is exactly what you must not go by. The feeling. You just go by the feeling and then you judge.

ALBERT. I see, I feel and I judge. I know about traps.

BENJAMIN. You won't listen. You won't hear. Those with ears, Albert, do you hear, let them hear. What I have to tell you, you with the fingers in your silly ears, what I have to tell you, listen, is not any particular fact, like what you've just been saying, and it's all the more valuable for that reason. It's not something anybody's ever seen or heard or come across or bumped into. It's not something you'd find out by keeping your eyes peeled or your ears open. Noses are no good. Your tongue couldn't taste it. But, Albert, and this is very impressive, it is true, universal and valid. It is wise. Yes. It is a part of wisdom and I'm going to tell you about it. Then you'll be easier, Albert.

ALBERT. I can't hear. Nothing. I can't hear.

BENJAMIN. Easier, Albert. You'd not be so upset. You'd be able to bear things; you wouldn't have horrible nightmares. You'd be able to bear things... like murder, rape, arson, and killing pigs and doing in a few million mice. (He laughs)

ALBERT. Then it's all bloody lies and I don't want to hear it. It's not wise, Benjamin, although you say it is. I'm an evil old bugger, Benjamin, and so are you. I do nasty things. But you're worse than me. You do nasty things for a reason. You have a theory about it.

BENJAMIN. If you won't bloody listen, you won't bloody learn.

ALBERT. I see, I feel and I judge. That's the right way

and no crackpot theory of yours is going to alter that.

BENJAMIN. (Loftily) Listen. This story is not a theory.
It's a conglomeration of facts properly understood,
that's all, presented, may I say, presented in such
manner as to pass the censors of your narrow brain
and enter into its own kingdom of truth; I mean, Albert,
the throne of reason, such as it is.

ALBERT. Tell it then. And when you've told it there will
be peace.

BENJAMIN. (With great satisfaction) Ehem... To begin.
Far away and forever far off, before sunrise, and all
that, before things slithered from the sea and men fell
like warm plumbs out of their wombs...

ALBERT. (Thinks of something else. Sadly) A nice
beginning.

BENJAMIN. Well, then... before there were insects and
crabs scuttling about all over the place, when the sky
was dark as armpits and no stars or wandering planets
were made, when, then, to cut a long story short, there
was nothing but pin points and huge spaces, when all of
this was the case... nothing mattered a tinker's
bugger. There was nothing but these meaningless
bloody grains and time, (Turning to ALBERT) Albert,
was simply the idea of gathering order. There was
nothing but the specks and space growing together into
shape and structure.

ALBERT. Shape and structure.

BENJAMIN. (Ignoring the interruption) Yes. Because there
was this growing shape and order and structure in all
things... and as this was so, so what was possibly so
and so, or this and that, became such and such, and
that and not this, as what was facing five ways, and
possible in more ways than we can count, became
simply a so and so, so, (Triumphantly) say I, and
alas, did death enter the world.

ALBERT. Ah, that was a sad thing to happen.

22

BENJAMIN. Necessary, Albert, essential, you see, since, as we well know, what's dead is done with, is finished, exhausted, utterly known and predictable. What is more sad, inert and predictable than the sullen immovability of the dead, dead fish on a slab... they no longer surprise or defeat us with a flicker or twist, or a dead dog, heaving with flies; (Turning to ALBERT) there, Albert, is order, exclusion of change, shutting the doors one by one, sealing off rooms of light and possibility, so that what is walks in one way.

ALBERT. (Mournfully, raising one leg) Like limbs getting stiff, face growing hard, legs treading the same way, only more and more slowly, dead set in your ways.

BENJAMIN. It is and it was so. Like water, in the beginning, fluent, unformed, shapeless; like water on a cold night freezing on glass, dead, silver structures, caskets, faces, fronds, crabs, conches, everything, all stiff and still and glittering white and dead. Dead, Albert, beautiful, white and still. Order, necessity, change. The visible face of time.

ALBERT. I see and behold it is true. History, Benjamin, is the dying of the world.

BENJAMIN. I conclude that death needs life and life needs death, like lines need points and points need lines, that if the law of change is death and if change is from the less to the more created who serves death serves creation. (He grunts)

ALBERT. (Looks sharply at BENJAMIN. They meet again) You mean laying traps, Benjamin, which is wrong and horrible and perverse and murderous and destructive.

BENJAMIN. The world is a butcher's shop.

ALBERT. The world is a place in which absolute goodness is possible.

BENJAMIN. The world, Albert, is a place in which pleasure-pain machines bump into each other and cry out or laugh.

ALBERT. Am I a pleasure-pain machine? No, I am not.

BENJAMIN. A pleasure-pain machine, with a feed-back, a nose for a good smell, an eye that looks into the future, fingers that grope round corners and legs to walk from one bloody catastrophe to another.

(They fade away from each other, as BENJAMIN develops his theme.)

ALBERT. (To himself) There is in me...

BENJAMIN. We'll eat anything, Albert... human beings'll eat anything. Rats, moles, goats, pigs, lambs, birds, fish, they'll sink their fangs into anything, Albert.

ALBERT. In me...

BENJAMIN. They'll bloody well tear at each other. They'll eat each other if they're hungry enough. They ravage and gnaw at their own kind.

ALBERT. There is in me...

BENJAMIN. We'll eat our way through the whole universe. The universe of man is filled with the sound of his jaws. Munch, munch, munch.

ALBERT. Something...

BENJAMIN. (Irritably) What? What?

ALBERT. Not seen or heard. Not touched.

BENJAMIN. Feeling without reason is blind. What is not seen or heard is nothing.

ALBERT. Reason without feeling is terrible.

BENJAMIN. Munch, munch, munch. You can hear that alright.

ALBERT. Shhh.

BENJAMIN. You can hear that alright.

ALBERT. There he is.

BENJAMIN. There is whom?

ALBERT. The Corporal.

BENJAMIN. Enter Victory and Defeat.

(The CORPORAL's voice is heard as he approaches the door.)

CORPORAL. Left, right, left, right. Pick up your feet there. Smartly. Party, party, HALT. Stand at ease. Stand EASY.

(He opens the door. He springs to attention, salutes. He is dressed as a corporal of the first world war. His uniform is stained and ragged but his boots are highly polished.)

CORPORAL. Stretcher party, ready and correct, sir.

ALBERT. Oh, God. Dismiss the chaps, Corporal.

BENJAMIN. I bet it was hell out there.

ALBERT. It's a wonder you got through.

CORPORAL. (He speaks as if delivering a report) Dropping like flies. R.T.O. can't cope with the casualties. Heavy bombardment... horses all shot beneath them, too much mud.

BENJAMIN. Many dead, then? How many dead?

CORPORAL. Some say thousands. Where I was there were many dead. Too many, too much for counting.

ALBERT. What was it like, then? Was it very bad?

CORPORAL. But for the smoke I would have seen every-thing. On the first morning...

25

BENJAMIN. At dawn...

ALBERT. As the sun was just under the hill, before there were sounds...

CORPORAL. ... the barrage began... tremendous... streamers of fire... laid down in lines, creeping in bursts of earth towards their lines...

BENJAMIN. The enemy...

ALBERT. Cold, shivering, grey faces...

BENJAMIN. Lick their lips...

CORPORAL. ... tearing great deep holes in the wire...

ALBERT. Watching... blinded by light and darkness...

BENJAMIN. ... shattered muscles, bones and blood...

CORPORAL. ... yes, a walking pillar of fire, a great whining, a constant roar and whistle of shells. We, gentlemen, had been roused and drunk our tea, you see, and we were standing in the fire trenches ready to go...

ALBERT. Then?

CORPORAL. It was all still... and we went over.

BENJAMIN. Lines of... lines of...

CORPORAL. A long line stretching to left and right, in perfect formation...

ALBERT. Perfect formation...

CORPORAL. Till they bloody started. Not saturated, their lines broke into fire, a constant, accurate and whitering fire, great gaps appeared, faces turning to left and right... I was shouting...

ALBERT. What?

CORPORAL. ... shouting... and so were they, we were
all shouting... but nobody heard nothing... they were
falling, the smoke was making me cough... and nobody
knew...

BENJAMIN. And some fell down holding their stomachs...

ALBERT. ... crying Jesus...

CORPORAL. ... then... suddenly... we were running...
back... back... it was all over...

ALBERT. ... the first morning.

BENJAMIN. ... a tragic defeat...

CORPORAL. A minor engagement... so it appears.

ALBERT. A hard life.

CORPORAL. It is that and no mistake. Though, gentlemen,
it isn't all blood and snots, not by any manner of means,
... no... not all bad... you see.

BENJAMIN. It has its moments.

CORPORAL. It has its moments, as you rightly remark.
The second morning, now...

ALBERT. Not so bad...

CORPORAL. Quite nice, really. We were resting, after the
day before and getting back into order... and it was
warm... that morning... people going about...

BENJAMIN. From place to place...

CORPORAL. Doing their own jobs... civilians... and
weren't bothering... just lying and talking and smoking
... and then...

BENJAMIN. You were all blown to bloody hell!

CORPORAL. (Indignantly) No we wasn't. Nothing like that.

27

(The possibility occurs to him. He is surprised.)

Though we might've been, come to think of it. We was in range. They could have got us. We was relaxing.

ALBERT. All talking and laughing...

CORPORAL. That is quite true... the sun... the sun...

BENJAMIN. Was...

CORPORAL. ... was very warm, you see, very nice and warm and the grass...

BENJAMIN. Was green!

CORPORAL. When, gentlemen... this was the best part... we heard in the distance...

ALBERT. Afar off, half heard...

BENJAMIN. As in a dream...

CORPORAL. Horses, by God, the sound of horses, trotting, lots of horses. We thought... horses, by God, horses, that's a funny thing.

ALBERT. Indeed.

BENJAMIN. What's funny about horses?

CORPORAL. (He is annoyed by the thought. Tries to explain) Horses, at that time, the line a sea of mud... the sun couldn't dry it... we never had thought of horses.

BENJAMIN. (Smiling) Never had thought of horses... no.

CORPORAL. And suddenly there they were, all these horses and riders, the riders in blue and scarlet, the horses caparisoned, trotting and jingling. So we gave them a cheer. We thought, horses, that's something though...

BENJAMIN. What, you could not say.

CORPORAL. We were happy to see them, but sad, you see, at the same time. They went past in perfect formation, in very good order...

BENJAMIN. In perfect formation, in good order. Yes, that's very good.

CORPORAL. Yes, it was good. In perfect order... their flanks were shining... their boots were perfectly polished.

ALBERT. Their eyes were large and their heads were turning, the riders rising and falling, the bodies beneath them... the sun was shining, there was a light about them...

CORPORAL. And then they were gone... we heard them, fading, and then they were gone.

BENJAMIN. That was the second morning.

CORPORAL. The second morning. On that morning, gentlemen, we fell quiet and saw the horses.

ALBERT. Was this rest long?

CORPORAL. Not very long, but we were quite rested. We moved that night, there being no moon, we moved.

BENJAMIN. Ghosts...

CORPORAL. Like ghosts, certainly, under cover of darkness. The order was, no sound.

BENJAMIN. But someone coughed...

ALBERT. Somebody stumbled...

CORPORAL. Somebody swore and was quietly reprimanded. We met our guide who took us into the line... a very bad section, a low lie, the enemy, from a slight rise could fire into the line.

BENJAMIN. And then there were rats.

CORPORAL. Rats. My Christ, you could hear them bloody rats, slithering about... splashing quietly into the water....

BENJAMIN. Which did reek.

CORPORAL. It stank, the water did. And there were arms and legs from the last barrage, or the one before that. Arms and legs, as grey as cold mutton. A bad section.

ALBERT. Did you have rest?

CORPORAL. We took it in turns. I had the go just before morning...

ALBERT. The third morning...

CORPORAL. Yes, the third morning... the third morning ... we went over... in grey light... mist on the water ... all very quiet... then...

BENJAMIN. Noise, noise, noise.

CORPORAL. Terrible, the sky torn to bits, flares rising and falling, machine guns testing the whole line...

ALBERT. You broke and came back.

CORPORAL. We bloody well didn't. We went on going, we went on going...

BENJAMIN. ... to the first trenches...

CORPORAL. (Savagely) And in we went, in, out, on guard, in, out, in, out, give 'im your butt, get him in the ghoolies. (More calmly) We got out our bayonets and cleared that first line.

ALBERT. Clutching his stomach, a wound as large as his arm, his fingers are fountains...

CORPORAL. We cleared that first line. Then through and

over... we were advancing...

BENJAMIN. Blood in your eyes, Corporal, on your boots, your legs all stained, your boots smeary with blood.

CORPORAL. The ground was rising. The thing is they had a system of second line trenches and then more trenches, a system in depth.

ALBERT. The enemy, those who were fighting and those you were fighting...

CORPORAL. We rounded this corner and came on a bunch of them, huddled together. We cleared that corner and came into an open field.

BENJAMIN. A place not to rest in.

CORPORAL. Not bloody likely. We meant to cross over and consolidate in the next line. That's when we saw them.

BENJAMIN. That's when you saw them.

CORPORAL. That's when we saw them, the horses. All smashed to pieces, all lying and broken, great black and brown horses, a whole field of dead horses.

ALBERT. Sick to your stomach...

BENJAMIN. Horses denied by battle.

CORPORAL. All those dead horses, eyes wide open or broken like...

BENJAMIN. Smashed statues.

CORPORAL. All broken... like... men. Like men. We hadn't thought of them horses as human.

BENJAMIN. Great bodies of meat.

ALBERT. Without riders. Like toys, in blue and gold and red, smeary with mud.

CORPORAL. That was the third morning. The enemy came over and over and we went back.

BENJAMIN. The grey line of marching bayonets... the shouts, the shrieks, the howls.

CORPORAL. That was the third morning... the death of the horses. All dead in that field. When we looked over... much later... we saw them all lying.

ALBERT. Like broken statues.

BENJAMIN. On the third morning.

ALBERT. The third morning.

CORPORAL. It's nice to be back.

(They stand, looking at one another. End of scene.)

ACT TWO

(Scene as before. ALBERT is on the sofa. BENJAMIN
is in the corner with his basket. The CORPORAL is
sitting on the trunk. He stretches himself and looks
round as if coming out of a dream.)

CORPORAL. Well, it's nice to be back.

BENJAMIN. You'll enjoy a bit of leave, you mad old bugger.

CORPORAL. That I will. And don't you forget it. That I
will. Don't you forget.

BENJAMIN. The man of war, weary with all his giant
labours, enjoys his merited rest. The titan rests.

ALBERT. We won't forget. As long as you don't make too
much bloody noise in your sleep, with cannonades and
ambuscades and shouting instructions and rolling about
and sweating and staring and diving under the bed, we
won't forget it.

CORPORAL. Libels, gentlemen. I never dream. Well
known for the innocence of me slumbers. Sleep like a
baby, just like a little baby, me. Eyes close, head
down and I'm off.

BENJAMIN. To hell and back in perfect formation.
Corporal dismiss.

ALBERT. There's a scratching at the door.

BENJAMIN. Them mice, then.

33

ALBERT. Mice don't whisper. There are whispers at the door. Everybody be quiet. Listen...

(They retreat to the back of the stage. GEORGE and MIRIAM are outside, trying to fit the key in the door.)

MIRIAM. Put it in, then.

GEORGE. I'm trying to, aren't I? Don't be so impatient. It's dark, isn't it? It's dark, isn't it? I can't see.

MIRIAM. Feel for it, then. Hurry up, George.

GEORGE. Don't be so impatient. You put it in then.

(Sound of key in door. They enter, still talking. They are dressed as any modern, youngish, about to be married couple of the upper working class would be dressed.)

MIRIAM. You mean it, George, don't you? This time, I mean, you really mean it. You're not just saying it? Like last time?

GEORGE. You know I mean it, pet. What d'you think we're looking at this house for? Of course, I mean it.

MIRIAM. Do you, though? D'you love us? Because last time you went all funny and that and you remember, last time, and if you don't mean it you should say so.

GEORGE. I can't say any more, now can I? I've said I will and I will. When I say something like that then I do it. Anybody that knows me'll tell you that, love. If you like this place we'll take it and that'll be that.

MIRIAM. I'll not be happy until we're in.

GEORGE. It'll not be for a bit yet, pet. You see, there's a lot to get done first, you know. It'll take a bit of time. It's no good rushing.

MIRIAM. Not all that long. We don't have to do everything at once, love. We could move in and then do it, you see.

34

We could do it bit by bit. If you wanted to, that is, if you really wanted to.

GEORGE. That cornice could do with a lick of paint. That's a long job for a start.

BENJAMIN. (Whispers) I told you. They're moving in.

ALBERT. They're not moving into my house. They are not moving into my house. Let that be said and let that be understood.

CORPORAL. They're setting up house. That's what they're doing. And this is the house they're setting up in.

BENJAMIN. They're going to be married.

ALBERT. In September, when the rain comes.

MIRIAM. Should we have a big wedding, George?

(While they are talking they should be moving about separately examining the room.)

ALBERT. Not here, you're not.

GEORGE. With bridesmaids and that, and your brother?

BENJAMIN. He's as good as married already.

ALBERT. Poor sod.

MIRIAM. He's quite nice, really, when you get to know him.

BENJAMIN. She'll have him for breakfast.

GEORGE. Where would you have it?

ALBERT. Terrify them away.

MIRIAM. In church, with flowers.

CORPORAL. He's a quiet one. Make a good N. C. O.

BENJAMIN. She's got a good rump on her. A lot of warm thoughts in her.

MIRIAM. This carpet'll have to go out.

CORPORAL. In Cairo...

GEORGE. And that sofa.

ALBERT. The Nile flows round the red walls and the sun burns the pavement.

BENJAMIN. In Cairo.

MIRIAM. (Bending over the sofa) It stinks.

CORPORAL. They're all blacks. Girls, rumps glossy as horses. The men are all black.

GEORGE. Some funny stones over here.

ALBERT. Black.

BENJAMIN. As black as arseholes, as nasty as nightmares

GEORGE. Miriam.

MIRIAM. What, pet?

GEORGE. Come and look at these stones.

ALBERT. Terrify them away.

CORPORAL. Black. And we were all white, you see. A terrible responsibility.

MIRIAM. What stones, love?

ALBERT. She's sitting on my sofa.

BENJAMIN. He's fiddling with your stones.

GEORGE. Stones, over here, by the window.

MIRIAM. Ooh, I am tired. That's three houses today. I'm absolutely exhausted, George.

GEORGE. What is it, love?

MIRIAM. I'm not half tired.

GEORGE. You should come and have a look at these stones. The chap that had this house must have had funny ideas. Fancy bringing stones in; big as well. Like enormous frogs, love.

MIRIAM. Frogs? What are you on about?

GEORGE. These stones, pet, like frogs.

ALBERT. (Creeping up behind the sofa and peering down at MIRIAM whose eyes are closed) Like little black men, dear. Do you hear me, little black men?

MIRIAM. Oh! (She twists restlessly) Little black men.

GEORGE. (Perplexed by the stones) Bloody funny.

ALBERT. Little black men.

MIRIAM. Black men. All smiling and lovely white teeth. Animals! Should all be chained up like dogs. Animals. Walking about. Talking, laughing at us. Black. Nasty black creatures. Nobody's safe. Lanes. Dark streets. Jumps out. At you. Grab you. Oh. Black. White teeth. I see you. Black man. Strong. Love. Oh. Black arm. Squeeze, squeezing. My love, my black love. Kiss. Love. Girl. Little white girl. So big. Oh. Love you, love you. Mmmmmm.

ALBERT. Sex. Sex.

MIRIAM. Animals. Marching. Oh. (She sleeps.)

GEORGE. What? What, love? (He comes round and looks at her) Poor kid. She's dead beat. She's asleep. Them stones. Funny thing to have in a house. Like an eastern religion. It's cold in this room.

(He sits on the carpet, resting his head on the side of the sofa.)

They do funny things at these ceremonies. Cut you. Initiations. Like Mau Mau's. Savages. Dropped out of trees. Like those baboons we saw in the zoo. Just like baboons. The women have funny backsides

ALBERT. Black. Marching.

GEORGE. (Nodding) They'll rise. (Starts) They'll rise, all over Africa. Yellow peril. Red menace. Black flood, rivers of black heads. All curly.

MIRIAM. Curly. Like lambs. Curly black heads. (She fondles GEORGE's head) My little black lamb. Baby.

GEORGE. Black. Black hands, on you. Grabbing you. Cut your throat. Errrrr. Cut it with a big knife. Blood. All over. Grinning at you. Negro, negro, negro. Get the women off the streets, out of the way. Swarm all over. Masters. Giving orders. Should be flogged. Beat me. Whips. Made of bull's pizzles. Whip, whip, whip.

ALBERT. As big as stars, their eyes. Minds like cess-pools.

GEORGE. They stink. Smell them a mile off. Giving me orders. Oh! I'm not strong. (Coughs) I've got a weak chest. Mummy says I've got a weak chest. Black masters. Yes. Negroes. Kings. My black lord, my nigger king. Say, say. I kneel. My lord. My king.

ALBERT. They're not living here.

BENJAMIN. They should be in bed.

ALBERT. Somebody should take care of them. They're not fit to be out.

BENJAMIN. Shoes made of cardboard.

ALBERT. Chemical clothes and plastic teeth. Material to be blessed.

CORPORAL. They're sleeping together.

ALBERT. Disgusting.

BENJAMIN. New, warm, white little creatures. Lifting a stone, they wriggle.

ALBERT. In the wrong place.

CORPORAL. They're looking for a place to settle down in.

ALBERT. Somewhere to settle. Babes in the wood.

BENJAMIN. Here come the wolves.

ALBERT. And bears.

BENJAMIN. And rats.

CORPORAL. (Ruminating) Resting in fields after battle the ants got under my trousers and marched up my legs. In perfect formation. First leg, second leg, third leg, fourth leg. Up my trousers and out at my neck. Very impressive. I was all wet. My best friend was dead. Head went with a cannonball, shot through the chest with an arrow. Three bullets tore holes in him. We lost that battle.

BENJAMIN. I'm not surprised.

ALBERT. Poor little beings. I'm telling you. They ought to be married and warm. And tucked up and not touched and left to themselves. More harm than good.

BENJAMIN. What are they for?

CORPORAL. The armed services. The Royal Regiment of foot. The mounted artillery. Ships of the line. Her... to...

ALBERT. Come home to.

BENJAMIN. A horrible prospect.

ALBERT. They ought to be taken care of. Somebody ought to make them into whatever it is easy for them to be.

BENJAMIN. Husband and wife.

ALBERT. Nine to five-thirty.

CORPORAL Marching and waltzing.

BENJAMIN. Cover their nakedness. They should be decently covered.

ALBERTO. They should be done out from top to toe. Scrubbed, scalded, cleaned out and dressed for the part.

(They nod to one another. BENJAMIN goes over to the trunk. He drags it over.)

BENJAMIN. Here, as you were saying, is the first garment.

(They crowd around. The box is opened and garments are produced. GEORGE and MIRIAM are dressed as bride and bridegroom.)

ALBERT. Don't they look splendid.

BENJAMIN. As good as new, as perfect as possible. Eh?

ALBERT. Stripped and scrubbed and bright as a pin. Reborn.

BENJAMIN. In the house of madness who will officiate?

(They begin to attire ALBERT like a priest)

ALBERT. In matters of ceremony

BENJAMIN. You take the biscuit

CORPORAL. I drink the beer.

BENJAMIN. I assist in a purely derisory capacity.

ALBERT. (Skipping forward and examining himself with pride) My tires, my mantles, my capes, tiaras, staffs, helmets, boots, and horn-rimmed spectacles.

BENJAMIN. You do look nice.

CORPORAL. One of the top ten if ever I saw one.

ALBERT. A credit to the community. Stand to one side. Make way. I go to my place.

(They draw aside the sofa and ALBERT goes and stands in front of the large balachite in the centre of the window. BENJAMIN and the CORPORAL are his acolytes.)

BENJAMIN. Not less than a bishop.

CORPORAL. A cardinal.

ALBERT. A pope.

BENJAMIN. What an honour.

ALBERT. You may kiss my ring.

BENJAMIN. Not with a bargepole.

ALBERT. Miriam, approach. White worms approach.

(They go forward slowly and face ALBERT. They should stand at a slight angle to the balachite.)

ALBERT. Miriam.

MIRIAM.. Yes.

ALBERT. Miriam. Little lovely bride, pretty little woman. Hear what I say.

MIRIAM. I am.

ALBERT. You are. What are you going to do when you get him?

MIRIAM. I'm going to gobble him all up until there's nothing left.

ALBERT. Repeat after me.

MIRIAM. I will.

ALBERT. You will. I, Miriam.

MIRIAM. I, Miriam.

ALBERT. I, Miriam, swear

MIRIAM. I, Miriam, swear

ALBERT. To love George and adore him.

MIRIAM. To love...

ALBERT. And adore him and to gobble him all up to the last delicious morsel of white skin and to defeat him and change him and transform him and to weaken him until the end of his days. Do you swear?

MIRIAM. I do.

ALBERT. Good. George.

GEORGE. Yes.

ALBERT. Speak when you're spoken to. George. (Silence) George. (Silence) Where the hell are you. Answer.

GEORGE. Here I am.

ALBERT. Standing before me, George, in your little white body and your tail. What will you do?

GEORGE. I will worship this sweet woman till the flesh falls from my bones and in the grave my green body will sprout flowers for her and all my lovely sons and children of her will walk over my grave and plant flowers there.

ALBERT. So they will. When they remember. Over this union of him and her I pronounce my blessing. May they cleave and cling, for ever and ever, and not be two but one, one heart, one heat, one flesh, one form, one brain, one body, one lust, one life, till all things fade for them and they go from the world. Who giveth this man?

CORPORAL. Me.

ALBERT. And who giveth this lovely sweet woman?

BENJAMIN. Me.

ALBERT. Then head to heart and hands over each other, a moist kiss to complete it. Kiss.

(They kiss.)

ALBERT. I now pronounce you ruin and strife. Clash and collide. For ever and ever, amen.

BENJAMIN. Strike up music. Let organs sound. Let choir boys sing and all that. Let the world rejoice. A marriage has been perpetrated. Now they will live in a likely and complacent manner, he her husband, she his wife.

GEORGE. I father.

MIRIAM. Me, mother.

ALBERT and BENJAMIN. Girl and boy.

CORPORAL. Mum and Dad.

ALBERT. One unit, one factory, one for each and each for each other.

BENJAMIN. To the end.

ALBERT. That spasm shall make child.

CORPORAL. To walk and war and marvel and make end.

(During this sequence and subsequent to the pronouncement of marriage ALBERT, BENJAMIN, the CORPORAL, GEORGE and MIRIAM form a blasphemous procession and proceed round the stage chanting.)

GEORGE. To live close and lovely and keep them all out.

MIRIAM. In my four warm walls, me and him and all them babies and us and them.

BENJAMIN. And he shall work.

MIRIAM. And I shall weep.

CORPORAL. But they will survive and thrive and not give a bugger.

ALBERT. And she shall be called woman.

BENJAMIN. And he man.

CORPORAL. The snake shall bruise their heels.

ALBERT. A likely story.

GEORGE. And when the baby is born

MIRIAM. Ooh, he'll milk me and we'll be so drowsy and tugging and my nipples stained with blood.

GEORGE. My proud, fat boy, my little cannibal. And he will name all the things, Mummy, Daddy, teddy, motor, fire, water, milk, coffee, beans and bread.

MIRIAM. And angels will watch over my sleeping baby darling and sing.

CORPORAL. And the angel will cut with his sword the red clouds and fire will stream from his mouth and the gates shall be opened and shut.

BENJAMIN. It stands to reason.

ALBERT. And falls by the wayside.

CORPORAL. They'll be frying tonight.

(ALBERT, BENJAMIN and the CORPORAL come
forward, speaking to one another. They lead GEORGE
and MIRIAM to the sofa. They remove their bridal
garments. GEORGE and MIRIAM assume the same
posture as before the ceremony)

BENJAMIN. In hell there would be green devils roasting
their twenty toes and two heads on the grills. And
racked from end to end the suffering people. One
screech for every second they breathe. Screech,
screech, screech.

ALBERT. If there were heaven the placid good ones would
all be arrayed in rows, singing their heads off. The
saved must be very musical.

CORPORAL. And in Limbo the scarlet jackets are
marching from morning till night; and the drums are
beating; colours are flying; the mock horses dance, the
generals take the salute, the cannons rock and thunder
over the yellow stone roads. And the sun never sinks
on the Empires of our desire.

ALBERT. In limbo where loving is green and cool as
April.

BENJAMIN. Where grey beards reason from one false
proposition to another, where the logic is impeccable.

CORPORAL. Where every man walks with a soldier's
bearing, where rank is respected, gentlemen, sirs,
where corporals stand to attention, where no-one is
insubordinate and where, when the sergeant shouts
they bloody well all come running.

ALBERT. Heaven, where love is transitive, reflexive and
where it exists.

BENJAMIN. Where human beings are faced with an endless
prospect of nightshirts and good behaviour, where
reality goes to the devil.

CORPORAL. We shall be nameless.

(GEORGE and MIRIAM wake.)

GEORGE. (Rubbing his eyes, stretching. Looks around.)
I must have dropped off, then.

MIRIAM. I wasn't half tired, George.

GEORGE. I bet you were, love.

(They stand up and look around.)

MIRIAM. Should we take it?

GEORGE. It'll need a lot of attention. I mean, them boards
and that. And that ceiling. And a lot of painting. That
door'll have to come down.

MIRIAM. It could be quite nice.

GEORGE. We'll have to think about it.

MIRIAM. There isn't much time.

GEORGE. It'll need a lot of attention.

(They are talking as they go towards the door. They
pause at the door, look around and go out.)

BENJAMIN. Well, they've gone, then.

CORPORAL. Yes, they've gone.

ALBERT. They ought to be wrapped up in bandages and fed
with a tube.

CORPORAL. That lady would do very well in an army
brothel.

BENJAMIN. What?

CORPORAL. That lady... nothing. I was just thinking
thoughts to myself.

ALBERT. I'm very tired. I am about to retire.

BENJAMIN. Yes. I am very tired.

CORPORAL. Lights out, then, gentlemen.

ALBERT. Not yet. I have a thing to do yet. You know that.

BENJAMIN. Not these bloody stones you're not. There will
be no bloody stones. We've had enough of this and that
and everything for one day.

CORPORAL. It's very late. It is very late indeed.

ALBERT. There must be stones. It's time for stones and
stones there will be. I am taking a stand.

BENJAMIN. Well, take it then and be damned to you.

ALBERT. Thank you.

BENJAMIN. I shall rest on the couch and the couch must
not be moved.

ALBERT. If you would be so good, Corporal.

CORPORAL. Always ready to oblige the authorities, as you
might say.

(The CORPORAL takes the foot of the couch and
ALBERT the head. They lift the couch across the stage
to stage right. As they do so BENJAMIN is staring at
them in high indignation. He raises his hand, turns
from one to the other. Then collapses back on the
couch.)

BENJAMIN. Thy will be done. But I'm not going to humour
you. I will ignore the whole business by snoring...
loudly, fit to wake the dead or rouse the living. You
have been warned.

(After the couch has been deposited ALBERT takes up a
position in front of the stones. The CORPORAL takes up
his stick and stands at ease by the door.)

ALBERT. Now then, there is to be the singing of the stones and I don't want anyone to make even a small sound, never mind snoring.

BENJAMIN. (Musing, as to himself) Birds can't speak, rats can't reason, flowers can't feel and stones can't sing.

ALBERT. Mmmm. Listen. Those with ears let them hear. To the ears of faith all things are possible.

BENJAMIN. The deaf hear no trumpets and the blind never imagine the glories of colour. If the impossible could happen everything would be true. Which it isn't.

ALBERT. Listen. I imagine the light. And there is light. I imagine the sound. And there is sound. There is sound and light and what I imagine is true. We shall then redeem the time. Memory will transfigure the past. The past will rise like a metaphysical grey bird to the sound of its own requiem.

BENJAMIN. Revolting rhetorical rubbish. Permutations of metaphysical hogwash and self-induced hypnosis.

ALBERT. (Takes up a book) Hush. It's beautiful. Listen. In the beginning made I heaven and earth, stars and everything...

BENJAMIN. I don't remember that!

ALBERT. And man and woman made I. In my own image. And they were beautiful.

BENJAMIN. They were what!

ALBERT. Beautiful. And the garden rose from the earth, bedecked...

BENJAMIN. Crikey!

ALBERT. With many birds and creature of many varieties.

(As he says this the lights change slowly. The music of

48

the stones begins. Since it is the music of stones let it be musique concrete. The scene is changing - light seems to stream through the window, sounds of birds and creatures are heard...)

BENJAMIN. (Puts his hand over his eyes) I don't believe it... I don't...

ALBERT. And looking around me, I was convinced that it was good.

BENJAMIN. Bad.

ALBERT. Good. And it was morning of the first day...

BENJAMIN. Oh, God...

ALBERT. And it was good...

(The musique continues. The scene ends.)

ACT THREE

(In the garden. There should be flowers and trees and
the whole should be flooded with a warm and perfect
light. The trees should be in fruit and each fruit must
be perfectly ripe. The flowers also should look perfect,
too perfect, as if they had never known change and
decay. To the left of centre there is a tree with apples
on it. The three balachites are ranged on stage right
to the rear of the stage. There is a notice beside the
tree, referred to later. The sky, of course, is blue.
Later the sky is to become a screen so there must be a
sufficiency of it visible to the audience. BENJAMIN is
sitting up in the tree. In this scene ALBERT,
BENJAMIN and the CORPORAL should appear obviously
as beings, slightly unreal. GEORGE and MIRIAM are in
a state of innocence but since most people are not they
may be allowed a light costume, possibly of a Greek
sort, or as little in the way of physical disguise as can
be ingeniously managed. Physically they should look
something like the pathetic and scrawny innocents of
Cranach's paintings of Eden. ALBERT and BENJAMIN
should be dressed as in Act I. The CORPORAL should
be dressed in denims and a forage cap.)

BENJAMIN. Good morning.

GEORGE. Good morning, thing.

BENJAMIN. Ah, you've had greetings then.

GEORGE. We had greetings yesterday. And today we have
    had more names. We did a lot of names this morning,
    thing.

BENJAMIN. What's my name, then? It's not very nice to call me a thing. Anything is a thing and when you talk to a thing you're not talking to anything, you know. It's not polite.

GEORGE. What's 'not polite'?

(He makes to go out)

BENJAMIN. Hi, where are you going?

GEORGE. I was going.

BENJAMIN. I know that. (Irritably) Idiots for company. That's his name, did he but know it. Where were you going?

GEORGE. Over the other side.

BENJAMIN. And then what?

GEORGE. Back again.

BENJAMIN. To the other side?

GEORGE. Yes. I suppose so.

BENJAMIN. And then what?

GEORGE. Do you really want to know?

BENJAMIN. No. Yes. I suppose so. I'm bored. It's not very pleasant, sometimes, being as important and clever as I am and nobody to be important to or cleverer than. I can't be cynical by myself. Yes, idiot, I really would like to know what you are going to do after you've been to the other side and back again.

GEORGE. (Enthusiastically) Well, you see, thing, I shall sit down and look up and then look down and stroke my stomach for a bit, because I like that, or she will, or I'll stroke hers, and then we'll go and look at... at...

BENJAMIN. What, what... what will you look at?

GEORGE. Flowers - I think. Yes, flowers and - what are they, er, brown, swaying about on the tops of the flowers?

BENJAMIN. Bees, bloody bees. Buzz, buzz, buzz. Buzzers, that's what they are. It's a stupid name 'bees'. Like calling something an 'is' or an 'are'. Bees.

GEORGE. Bees. Good. And being 'polite' then, what is your name, creature?

BENJAMIN. (Importantly) Now, thin white thing, know this, namely, that my name is Ben... ja... min, Ben... ja... min... Benjamin. Benjamin. (He calls out in a loud voice) BENJAMIN. (Reply comes 'Benjamin'.) From the far corners of the earth my name echoes.

GEORGE. Excuse me.

BENJAMIN. It reverberates. The stoats hear it. The rabbits remark it. Owls nodding trees hoot and answer. Yes?

GEORGE. Excuse me. What is my name?

BENJAMIN. Your name. Well... well... that is rather difficult, rather difficult to say really. Not really something I could divulge. What do you think it is?

GEORGE. (Promptly) George.

BENJAMIN. Well, goddam and blast it, if you knew what were you asking for?

GEORGE. Just to make sure, that's all.

BENJAMIN. I see. Well, George, what would you say to...

GEORGE. Goodbye.

(He turns and goes out)

BENJAMIN. Damn. Mmmm. Nothing to do but brood. Such tedium.

(Enter ALBERT, dressed as gardener, leading MIRIAM, garlanded with flowers.)

ALBERT. So it's this way today, my lady love, my young and beautiful queen, is it? This way today.

MIRIAM. Yes it is. Now move out of the way, old being, do.

ALBERT. Yes, my haughty darling. I will. (Catching BENJAMIN's eye) Aha. Aha. What are you doing in there?

BENJAMIN. Sickening vomit. Disgusting verbiage. My lady love, my young and beautiful queen. My dusky rose. My pink and preening creature. My shitting and farting animal.

ALBERT. (Angrily) What, what, what are you doing there?

BENJAMIN. Nothing. Just sitting. Just sitting in this silly garden waiting for petals to fall.

ALBERT. (Alarmed) What, where? Which petals? They can't.

BENJAMIN. Waiting, I said. Oh God. (He yawns) Roses forever crimson on green stalks, apples ripe for ever, grass that doesn't fade, a simple round sun to beam and beam and beam. Waiting, waiting.

ALBERT. What about the notice?

(He turns the notice round)

ALBERT. The notice says - Please do not enter. Penalty for improper use.

BENJAMIN. Well, I could do with some improper use. Penalise me, then.

ALBERT. Doesn't matter, really. You don't matter. It's them I worry about. So pure, so young, so innocent. Lambs they are. Knowing only truth, beauty and

53

goodness.

BENJAMIN. Nothing. She knows nothing. (Turning to
MIRIAM) You. What did you do today?

MIRIAM. I bathed in the blue fountain. I tended my hair,
and made it coil on my head. I laughed at three...

(She cannot remember. ALBERT interrupts and prompts
her)

ALBERT. Butterflies.

MIRIAM. Butter...flies. And I made myself a garland.

BENJAMIN. How could you bear the excitement?

MIRIAM. And now I must go and look for him. He must be
near the West side by now.

BENJAMIN. Wait. Come here.

ALBERT. Not too close now. Not too close, my dear.
Remember the notice.

MIRIAM. I remember, old being. What do you want, brown
thing?

BENJAMIN. Let me whissssper in your ear.

MIRIAM. What?

BENJAMIN. A lovely, lovely, lovely secret.

ALBERT. (Alarmed) There aren't any secrets.

BENJAMIN. Yes, there are. Lovely secrets. Let me
whisper.

MIRIAM. Alright then.

(He whispers. He must breathe into her ear and glance
down at her body as he whispers)

MIRIAM. No! No! (She giggles) I, I.

(She looks at herself. BENJAMIN starts to whisper more vehemently)

ALBERT. That's enough, I tell you. Enough.

MIRIAM. (She begins to look at herself) Breasts. What? Yes?

BENJAMIN. (More loudly) If you were just to come in here.

(GEORGE wanders in)

GEORGE. There you are, then. I was looking for you.

MIRIAM. Were you now. (She is flustered) Not looking very hard then, or you'd have found me.

GEORGE. How do you mean, love?

MIRIAM. George.

GEORGE. Miriam.

MIRIAM. George. I've got something to tell you, which this brown creature told me.

GEORGE. That's Benjamin.

ALBERT. Who told you that? He's an old...

BENJAMIN. What? Say it.

ALBERT. You shouldn't heed him. He's nothing.

BENJAMIN. I am something. I am here, on this bleeding endless, eternal apple branch. I am here. And I am me and my name is Benjamin. What's your name?

ALBERT. For the purposes of the present and without regard to what may or may not eventuate I am to be referred to an all subsequent occasions, unless otherwise stated and countermanded, as...

BENJAMIN. Albert.

ALBERT. As good as any other.

BENJAMIN. And not worse than most.

(Enter CORPORAL whistling)

CORPORAL Morning all.

ALL. Good morning.

BENJAMIN. Hello, Corporal.

CORPORAL. Hello, sir. And goodday to you, sir, and to
these two peculiar ones.

MIRIAM. Why does he say that, George?

GEORGE. Oh, him! He's funny, he is. He thinks we
should be walked to water and that in column, like he
does to others.

MIRIAM. What, us? Walked to water.

GEORGE. Yes. He's always walking groups of them about.

CORPORAL. (Cheerfully) Just finished the voles. Very
poor creatures, voles. Ants are good, though.
(Delighted with the idea) Walk themselves they will,
one day, see if they don't. You can see them practising.
I've seen them. Practising.

ALBERT. Time for rain.

MIRIAM. Not already.

ALBERT. Time for rain. I can smell it.

GEORGE. I like rain.

MIRIAM. I like rain, sometimes. But it makes my hair all

wet.

BENJAMIN. Spoils it. Rain.

CORPORAL. Could lead to mud.

ALBERT. Mud. Not here it won't. Not if I can help it.

(He addresses GEORGE, as a teacher might)

ALBERT. What is rain?

GEORGE. (Mechanically) Rain is good.

ALBERT. What are trees?

MIRIAM. (Mechanically) Trees are bad.

ALBERT. What? What's that?

MIRIAM. (Flustered) I mean...

ALBERT. Well?

MIRIAM. I mean... How do I know? Standing up. Great
thick things.

ALBERT. Trees are?

MIRIAM. Trees are good.

ALBERT. Standing is good.

MIRIAM. Yes.

GEORGE. Yes. Good.

ALBERT. Thickness is good.

MIRIAM. Thickness is... good. Yes.

ALBERT. Good. What is bad, then?

GEORGE. Nothing.

ALBERT. And nothing?

GEORGE. Is nowhere.

ALBERT. Tell her that. That is the lesson.

GEORGE. (Adopting superior tone) Well, Miriam. What is bad?

MIRIAM. Bad. Bad is nothing.

GEORGE. And nothing is nowhere.

MIRIAM. And nothing is... nowhere. George?

GEORGE. Yes, love.

MIRIAM. What is nowhere?

ALBERT. (Interrupts) Nowhere is not here. Outside, away, beyond. NOT. Nowhere is not.

MIRIAM. Oh!

ALBERT. Now...

(He turns towards the sky. He waves his arms)

ALBERT. Let there be creatures.

(The screen at the back is to produce shadows of creatures. They appear when the first creature is named. They must move rather jerkily across the screen, suggesting that they are being manipulated or even carried.)

BENJAMIN. If there are going to be creatures again, I'm going.

ALBERT. Nobody's stopping you.

BENJAMIN. Creatures. Gut bags. Makes me sick. Gone!

(He slides down the tree, grins and bares his teeth)

BENJAMIN. Grrr. I'll...

ALBERT. Now!

BENJAMIN. Eat you.

(He disappears)

ALBERT. Oh dear, oh dear.

MIRIAM. What is eat?

ALBERT. Passage and transformation of material from
one form to another. Chemical process. You know that.

GEORGE. I know that. Don't I? I know that, Miriam. So
do you, dear.

MIRIAM. Yes. Eat. What, then?

GEORGE. You know. We open our mouths and breathe in
air.

MIRIAM. That's eating?

ALBERT. In a sort of way it is.

CORPORAL. Duties. Must be on my duties. Got creatures
to sort out. They get mixed, you know. Found a weasel
in the rabbits the other day. Can't have that.

ALBERT. (Absentmindedly) No... indeed. No.

CORPORAL. Off then. (Clicks his heels) Sirs. Madam.

(He marches off)

ALBERT. He likes to sort things. (Thinks) Mmmmmm.
(Rouses himself) Well, then, people. Creatures.
Begin.

(A large bear appears, followed by other creatures)

GEORGE. Bear.

ALBERT. Correct.

MIRIAM. Vixen.

ALBERT. Correct.

GEORGE. Kangaroo.

MIRIAM. Brontosaurus. I've never <u>seen</u> one of them.

ALBERT. There aren't any... yet.

GEORGE. Seal.

ALBERT. Correct. Now listen.

(He reels off the names in ringing tones, becoming intoxicated with this march of creation, like a ring master announcing the various acts in a circus.)

ALBERT. Here come the sharks. Armadillos. Spiders. Next. Next.

(He peers anxiously)

Ah. Yes. Wait a minute, oh, yes. A flea. Now ladies and gentlemen, the sea lions, the tigers, the elephants proudly walking, the march of creatures.

(They begin to share his enthusiasm. They become fascinated by the spectacle like children.)

GEORGE and MIRIAM. Hurrah, hurrah.

ALBERT. And more. Mice, rats, giraffes, okapis, bats, eagles, lambs, so gently walking, great beasts now, tremendous creatures, gorrillas,' wolves, cats, moles, creeping close to the soil, badgers, stoats, buffaloes, thunder at their heels. More, more, more, more, let the interstices of heaven be filled, from great to small, ladies and gentlemen. Watch and wonder.

(As he says this the tide of creatures grows and swells across the screen.)

GEORGE and MIRIAM. Good, good.

ALBERT. And now?

GEORGE and MIRIAM. What?

ALBERT. Watch.

> (The screen darkens and then lightens. Two small
> lumps uncoil, extend, rise, raise their arms, bow to
> each other, take each other's hand and walk slowly,
> slowly across the whole screen.)

GEORGE and MIRIAM. What? What?

ALBERT. (Triumphantly) Man. Man. Humans. Walking.
Meeting. Recognising. Walking away.

GEORGE and MIRIAM. Us. There we are.

ALBERT. In it and not in it. Yes.

GEORGE and MIRIAM. Good, good, good.

> (The rain begins to fall. The screen darkens. A slight
> wind begins to blow.)

ALBERT. The end now. Sleep. Rest and sleep.

MIRIAM. (Tired, leans on GEORGE) Sleep. Tired. So
tired, George.

GEORGE. Yes, love. Sleep.

> (They walk off together. The lights go out. End of
> scene. When the lights go up again BENJAMIN is back
> in his tree.)

BENJAMIN. Creatures. A few bloody mouldy old arche-
types. Stuffed owls and moulting chickens, a few stray
tabbies, a rabbit or two and he's off. Creation, he
shouts, the march of creation. What an imagination.
Bloody miserable circus. Plod, plod, plod. (He flicks
his fingers) The blue-arsed baboon, the coleoptera,

the lepidoptera. Homo Sapiens, homo sapiens. Alright, Corporal. You can come out. You can give over. Where are you, you old villain.

(He looks behind the tree. Goes over to the screen)

Corporal in the sky, sublime swadi, come out.

(To himself)

Killed himself staggering over with that bloody gorilla on his shoulders. I wonder how he does that bit with the humans. Never mind. Doesn't matter. (Shouts) Hide if you want to. Lie doggo. I know you're bloody well there.

(Sees MIRIAM and GEORGE sleeping)

Ah. Aren't they lovely. Little snoozing doves.

(He raises his foot)

No.

(Looks down at them. Examines their faces)

Smooth as a baby's bottom. No lines. Experience writes not here. They don't know nothing. What's the world for them? Here and now. No memory but their own. A catalogue of kinds. Ignorant. (He stirs MIRIAM with his foot) Here you. You. Wake up. Woman. Girl. Female. Arise.

(She stirs, rubs her eyes. Looks up. Smiles)

MIRIAM. Oh, it's you, is it?

BENJAMIN. It's me, alright. Get up.

MIRIAM. What for?

BENJAMIN. Never you mind.

MIRIAM. Shall I wake him?

BENJAMIN. Him? No. Let him snore.

MIRIAM. Snore?

BENJAMIN. Making a sound through his nose.

MIRIAM. Oh, that. That's snoring, is it?

BENJAMIN. It is.

MIRIAM. Hmmmm. Let him snore then.

BENJAMIN. Listen, my dear, I've got something very nice for you.

MIRIAM. FOR me? How do you mean?

BENJAMIN. I mean for yourself. For you. Not them. Something for you, yourself. Not for the others. What they won't have.

MIRIAM. I see. You mean he won't have it?

BENJAMIN. Not him. Not nobody. Just you. That'll be nice?

MIRIAM. Nice? Yes. No. It's silly. Why not him?

BENJAMIN. Him. He wouldn't know what to do with it if he had one.

MIRIAM. Yes, he would. George is clever. He'd know if I told him.

BENJAMIN. Never mind him for one bloody minute. Think about yourself.

(MIRIAM frowns, ponders)

BENJAMIN. What are you doing now?

MIRIAM. Thinking.

BENJAMIN. Thinking?

MIRIAM. About myself.

BENJAMIN. And what did you find out?

MIRIAM. Nothing. I thought and thought but I didn't think anything.

BENJAMIN. Ah. That's it, you see. Not anybody can think about themselves. It's very difficult. It's very rare. Yes. Very rare indeed. Watch.

MIRIAM. What?

BENJAMIN. I'm thinking about myself.

MIRIAM. What are you thinking?

BENJAMIN. Thoughts nobody else has. I say, these are my thoughts and nobody else has these thoughts. So thinking these thoughts I think about me, you see. Do you understand?

MIRIAM. Yes, I think so. You have...

BENJAMIN. Well?

MIRIAM. (Triumphantly) Secrets.

BENJAMIN. That's it. Secrets. Thoughts, things that are only mine. And the more there is of mine, the more there is of myself, you see. You, Miriam...

MIRIAM. Yes?

BENJAMIN. You are as small as a point.

MIRIAM. Am I?

BENJAMIN. Yes. You only look outwards. Inside there's nothing.

MIRIAM. Liar.

BENJAMIN. Aha.

MIRIAM. Well. I do have things inside. I do have secrets.

BENJAMIN. Such as what?

MIRIAM. Well. Listen.

(She whispers)

BENJAMIN. Mmmm. Mmmm. Aha. Aha. I told you that.

MIRIAM. Well, what if you did? He doesn't know it.

BENJAMIN. True. Well, I suppose you do have secrets.
But secrets aren't enough.

MIRIAM. Really.

BENJAMIN. Really. Secrets are just the beginning. Actions
are what count.

MIRIAM. Actions are just doing things.

BENJAMIN. More. More. Much more than that. Actions
are much more than that.

MIRIAM. Actions are just walking and sitting down and
singing and things like that.

BENJAMIN. Actions are...

MIRIAM. Actions are?

BENJAMIN. Daring to do something. Watch. This is what
I call an action.

MIRIAM. You're going into that place.

BENJAMIN. That is the first action.

MIRIAM. It says not.

BENJAMIN. But I dare to do it. Do you, my love? Do you?

MIRIAM. No.

BENJAMIN. Now watch.

MIRIAM. Oh. That's horrible. You've torn an apple off
that tree.

BENJAMIN. I have. That is the second thing I dare do.

MIRIAM. What now, then? I don't like these actions.

BENJAMIN. Watch.

(He takes the apple and bites into it. She gives a shriek.
He munches it very noisely. He makes a meal of it. The
juice runs down his chin. He picks his teeth and chews
the bits. He eats the apple with relish down to the core.)

There.

MIRIAM. Oh, that's horrible. You sank your teeth into it.
You put it into your mouth. You bit it. You broke it.
You tore its nice skin.

BENJAMIN. I ate it.

MIRIAM. That's eating?

BENJAMIN. That's eating.

MIRIAM. But what about the apple? What about that?

BENJAMIN. It's inside me.

MIRIAM. (Fascinated) Inside?

BENJAMIN. Yes. I've swallowed it and now it's part of me.
Part of the world that wasn't me now is, you see. I'm
bigger. When I am biggest I'll have swallowed the world.

MIRIAM. That's eating, is it?

BENJAMIN. That's only the beginning. Tomorrow I'll catch
a lamb and kill it and roast it and we'll eat that.

MIRIAM. You beast. You won't.

BENJAMIN. Yes, I will. Lamb cutlets are delicious. And Miriam...

MIRIAM. What?

BENJAMIN. I might decide to eat you.

(She shrieks)

MIRIAM. You wouldn't dare.

BENJAMIN. (Rising in a rage) No? What? Wouldn't dare. I dare... anything. I can call things from the ground, black things, nightmares in daylight. I can dare anything. Do you hear, ANYTHING.

MIRIAM. (Hastily) Alright. I believe you. Don't shout.

BENJAMIN. Alright then.

(Pause. They look at each other. They grin)

I lost me temper.

MIRIAM. You did that.

BENJAMIN. But listen, it's right what I say. Do you want to see something.

MIRIAM. Well...

BENJAMIN. Exciting, new, strange, never before seen by man, woman or beast; fury and chaos rising and crying out of a man's brain. Would you like to see what I have stored there?

MIRIAM. Where?

BENJAMIN. In his brain. In your brain. This is where he is. This is where you are. This is what you possess and do not possess, the dark side of his moon, the shadowy disc of Venus, never observed.

MIRIAM. What difference will it make, seeing that. I mean,

would it just be more secrets?

BENJAMIN. More, much more. All the difference in the
world, you see. After this, well, you'll be much more
of yourself. Much more. You'll be so hard and
different from everything you'll hardly be able to think
of anything else, there'll be so much of yourself to
think of. Everything will be either you or not you and
everything will either become you or not become you.
You will...

MIRIAM. I will...?

BENJAMIN. Eat up the world.

MIRIAM. Me?

BENJAMIN. You and him. You'll see. You'll lash out at it
and devour it and it will lash out at you.

MIRIAM. That's silly. Why will it do that?

BENJAMIN. Because it isn't you and you aren't it. It'll
make huge bumps and bruises and snap necks and be
conquered and make war.

MIRIAM. It sounds... not very pleasant.

BENJAMIN. Not very pleasant.

MIRIAM. He's sleeping. Isn't he? Don't people look funny
when they're sleeping. Away. Somewhere... not here.
Bad, I suppose.

BENJAMIN. He looks funny when he's sleeping. That's
because when he's sleeping all the emptiness and air
inside pours out of his open mouth and his eyes are shut
on the vacancy of his mind. When he sleeps he is a body
breathing.

MIRIAM. What are you when you sleep, then?

BENJAMIN. Torn and twisted and fighting old battles. Like
the Corporal, wincing at old wounds.

MIRIAM. Is that better?

BENJAMIN. It is something.

GEORGE. Mmmm. (He mutters)

MIRIAM. He's stirring.

BENJAMIN. So that's what it is.

MIRIAM. Yes, he's stirring.

GEORGE. Oh. Yes. Oh. Ahhh.

BENJAMIN. George. George.

GEORGE. Yes. (Still half asleep) What, then. Trees are
   ... good. Snails are good.

BENJAMIN. George. Switch off a minute. Attend, George.
   Concentrate, George. George. Do you see the sky over
   there, George.

GEORGE. The sky. Yes.

BENJAMIN. And George, in that sky what do you see?

GEORGE. In the sky I see...

BENJAMIN. What do you see?

GEORGE. A cloud.

BENJAMIN. What sort of cloud.

GEORGE. Just an ordinary, pleasant white cloud. Round
   and white and puffed and...

BENJAMIN. Yes...

GEORGE. Moving.

MIRIAM. Clouds are good. George, remember.

GEORGE. Of course clouds are good. I know that.

BENJAMIN. What are clouds?

GEORGE. Clouds...

BENJAMIN. Clouds are vapour.

GEORGE. That's not the answer!

BENJAMIN. Look at the sky. The sky. Look at the sky. Look.

GEORGE. I am looking.

(The sky darkens. Four shadowy men. It is a night scene.)

1. Who're you pushin' man. Who... who... who... you pushin' man?

2. Ah'm not pushin' anybody, boy.

3. You're pushin' me, man.

4. Yeah, he's pushin' you.

2. Ah'm not pushin' anybody, boy.

(Fade to couples dancing. Slow blues.)

1. Mmmmm.

2. Mmmmmm.

1. Mmmmm.

2. Mmmmm.

3. Your table is ready now, sir.

4. What?

3. Your table is ready now, sir.

4. What?

3. Sir.

4. What?

3. Sir.

4. What?

(Fade to two boxers in shadow fight. One is beating hell out of the other in a corner. Crowd roars.)

CROWD. Aaaah. Aah. Aah.

ANNOUNCER. He's down. He's down.
One, two, three, four, five.

(Fade to night lights again. Cars, people passing; hoots, squeals of tires, clanging of bells.)

MIRIAM. What's their names.

BENJAMIN. This is a town, darlings.

GEORGE. Is it? A town?

MIRIAM. That's funny. That's nice.

BENJAMIN. Yes, darlings. Isn't it sweet. Darlings. This is a town. Ooh. It's lovely.

GEORGE. It's a town, then.

BENJAMIN. Yes. That's what it is.

MIRIAM. It's a town. I like it. I like that town.

BENJAMIN. Do you like it, George?

GEORGE. Yes...s. I think I like it. No. All those humans. Who are all those humans?

(Fade to two men sitting at a table. They are dividing

something. They speak in tones of bloodcurling venom.)

1. This is mine and this is yours.

2. This is his and this is hers.

1. That is theirs and this is ours.

2. This is my stone.

1. This is my plant.

2. This is my soil.

1. This is my head.

2. This is my head.

1. My head.

2. My legs.

1. My hair.

2. My nails.

1. My bowels.

2. My mouth.

1. Mine, theirs.

2. Yours, ours.

1. Ours, his.

2. Hers, theirs.

1. Give.

2. Take.

1. Get.

2. Want.

1. Have.

2. Got.

1 and 2. All, all, all. Got you, you bastard. Ha, ha, ha, ha, ha.

(Fade to man hanging on a branch or gibbet. He swings round. He raises his hands to his mouth. He plays a melancholy tune. As he turns in the slight wind the tune fades away and then returns. All three stare at him. They make what might be a slight obeisance. The sky grows blue again.

BENJAMIN. New ones. New humans. George. Miriam.

GEORGE and MIRIAM. Yes. What?

BENJAMIN. All those humans do what they like.

MIRIAM. (Suddenly) Apples.

GEORGE. (Points to the tree) There are apples.

MIRIAM. He ate one.

GEORGE. Apples are... What did you say?

BENJAMIN. I ate one.

MIRIAM. He did. Yes. He took one and ate it.

GEORGE. How d'you mean, ate it?

MIRIAM. (On impulse) Like this.

(She tears off an apple and munches it noisely)

Oooh. It's nice. It's all funny on my tongue.

BENJAMIN. It tastes good.

73

GEORGE. It's not supposed to happen. What are you doing? You've... broken it.

MIRIAM. Eat.

BENJAMIN. Yes, eat.

MIRIAM. Eat, George, eat. Put it in your mouth, love. Bite it.

GEORGE. Me? No.

MIRIAM. Eat. Munch it. Press your teeth in it.

GEORGE. What about...?

BENJAMIN. What?

GEORGE. (Weakly) That notice.

BENJAMIN. What notice?

GEORGE. That one, that one.

BENJAMIN. That notice. It's nothing. That notice.

(He takes the notice and smashes it.)

GEORGE. (Suddenly excited) Hurray. Smash it. Me. Me.

(He tears off an apple, then another. He stamps on them. He bites one and throws the rest away.)

GEORGE. Eat, eat. I'm eating. Eat those apples. Break them. Smash them. Smash that tree.

(They attack the tree. They beat at it with the remains of the notice. Suddenly they both stop. They stare at each other.)

GEORGE. You.

MIRIAM. You.

GEORGE. Why did you?

MIRIAM. Why did you?

GEORGE. You did first.

MIRIAM. Yes, I did. You smashed the tree.

GEORGE. I'll smash you.

MIRIAM. You dare.

GEORGE. I'll smash you. I'll beat you. I'll break your fingers. I'll eat you.

MIRIAM. What love? I'll eat you.

GEORGE. (Cunningly) Will you, now.

MIRIAM. Yes. (She slowly puts out her tongue) See.

GEORGE. Here, Miriam?

MIRIAM. George?

GEORGE. Love.

MIRIAM. Love.

GEORGE. Eat you.

MIRIAM. Gobble you all up.

GEORGE. Come, Miriam, Miriam.

MIRIAM. Come, George.

(They walk off together, leaving the ruins of the tree. Enter ALBERT, whistling. He stops. He stares. He goes over and picks up an apple. He looks at it, tries to polish it on his trousers. Looks at the tree. Tries to put the apple back on the tree.)

BENJAMIN. Irreversible event.

ALBERT. Yes. Them?

BENJAMIN. Yes, them.

ALBERT. Well. Where are they now?

BENJAMIN. Eating each other.

ALBERT. Are they? They'll find it troubles their stomachs.

BENJAMIN. They'll belch alright.

ALBERT. Yes. A lovely tree.

BENJAMIN. (Sadly) Yes, it was.

ALBERT. It'll all go now.

(Enter CORPORAL, excited)

CORPORAL. That weasel. That bloody old weasel. He's had a rabbit and tore its throat out.

ALBERT. It'll all go, now.

BENJAMIN. Better.

ALBERT. Worse.

BENJAMIN. Worse and better.

CORPORAL. The light's going.

ALBERT. It's getting dark.

(The sound of howling. A great cry goes up)

ALBERT. They are afraid.

BENJAMIN. They know terror.

CORPORAL. Looks like a storm.

ALBERT. The sky's in ruins.

(Rain begins to fall. The sound of animals, roaring, trumpeting. Wings are heard.)

ALBERT. The beasts are leaving.

(GEORGE and MIRIAM appear. They rush to the centre of the stage. They look round. They do not seem to see BENJAMIN, ALBERT or the CORPORAL.)

BENJAMIN. Humans.

ALBERT. Are good.

GEORGE. Miriam.

MIRIAM. George. George, I can't see.

(They stare wildly. They are dressed in the same clothes as in the first act.)

GEORGE. I can't see. Here. Here.

(There is a flash of lightning. They see each other. They stare at each other. GEORGE holds out his hands. They clasp hands. They walk around slowly. They pick up branches, then drop them. They walk out slowly.)

ALBERT. Going.

BENJAMIN. Going.

CORPORAL. Gone, ladies and gentlemen. Gone.

(They go over to the branches. They each pick up a branch)

ALBERT. Let there be music. Eh...? Shall we?

BENJAMIN. Huh!

CORPORAL. Lights out, gentlemen.

(The lights dim. ALBERT, BENJAMIN and the CORPORAL reverse branches and lean on them as in

mourning. The three stones light up. They form a
triad as do ALBERT, BENJAMIN and the CORPORAL.
As the last post sounds, first the CORPORAL's light
goes out, then BENJAMIN's and finally ALBERT's.
And with each light going out so the figure associated
with it is lost in darkness. The light, therefore, shows
ALBERT last. It fades with the music. The stage is
dark. Pause... The music fades, becomes a back-
ground...)

BENJAMIN. Where are we?

ALBERT. Here.

BENJAMIN. (Irritably) But where's here?

CORPORAL. In this place.

BENJAMIN. But where's that, for God's sake?

ALBERT. I don't know. It looks like the room.

BENJAMIN. The room?

ALBERT. A room, then.

CORPORAL. At a certain time...

ALBERT. In a certain condition...

BENJAMIN. (Is heard to move) Ouch... mmm... outside
it looks like people are walking in streets...

CORPORAL. Cats are parading in cohorts and squalling
choirs...

ALBERT. Dogs are yelping...

CORPORAL. Guns are going off... all over...

ALBERT. It looks like

BENJAMIN. Where we are...

ALBERT. Wherever that is...

CORPORAL. Somewhere slightly orf centre...

ALBERT. To the right of Acturus...

BENJAMIN. In full view of Orion...

CORPORAL. Observed by Riga...

ALBERT. In a small room...

BENJAMIN. Extremely non-commodious...

ALBERT. Ghosts... apparently... haunting...

BENJAMIN. In the back rooms of nowhere...

CORPORAL. In the presence, gentlemen, of an enormous, inexplicable balls-up...

ALBERT. Occasion...

BENJAMIN. Happening...

ALBERT. If they come back...

BENJAMIN. Who?

ALBERT. George...

BENJAMIN. Gawd!

CORPORAL. And that young female...

ALBERT. How will they live...

BENJAMIN. As best they can...

ALBERT. Benjamin?

BENJAMIN. What?

ALBERT. Am I a lunatic...

BENJAMIN. Who's to say...

ALBERT. Quite right... Benjamin?

BENJAMIN. What now?

ALBERT. I believe I'm asleep.

BENJAMIN. Good.

ALBERT. Is it?

BENJAMIN. I'm not sure... aaaaah.

(The musique rises... the curtain closes. The end.)

THE STRANGE CASE
OF
MARTIN RICHTER

THE STRANGE CASE OF MARTIN RICHTER was first performed on 8 November 1967 by the Citizens' Theatre Company at the Close Theatre Club, Glasgow. The play was directed by Michael Blakemore with the following cast:

MARTIN RICHTER	Martin Miller
HANS MUELLER	Del Henney
GOMBRICH	Robert Cartland
HEMMEL	Richard Kane
MARIE	Barbara Ewing
FRANZ GÜMMEL	Roy Boutcher

SCENE ONE

(A study. A large desk at right, on the wall at rear
an oil painting of a middle-aged, smiling, comfortable
man. A few books on the bookshelf. An armchair, etc.
A very comfortable room, verging on opulence, but
everything rather solid and heavy. MARTIN RICHTER
is standing contemplating the portrait; he is a somewhat rotund person, balding, wearing a dark suit.
Seated at the desk, a fresh-faced, fair-haired young
man, neatly attired. This is HANS MUELLER. As the
curtain opens the 'Horst Wessel' song is playing,
rather faintly. They stand or sit still until it is
completed. When they speak it should be in those
accents which people affect as versions of a German
accent.)

RICHTER. (Turns from the portrait, smiles) Well.
(Pause) I'm very pleased, Hans, with the way things
are going.

(When the music stops HANS begins to sort through
some papers. When RICHTER speaks he does not look
up)

HANS. You have every reason to be so, Herr Richter.

RICHTER. Every reason to be so, my pedantic Hans.

(Burst of cheering from the next room)

Gombrich will be in in a moment, you'll see.

HANS. A worthy fellow, Heinrich Gombrich. (Twists his
head on one side, bends forward. Speaks thickly) By

God, Herr Richter, HERR Richter, things are going well, very well.

RICHTER. (Smiling) That will do, Hans. Your mimetic propensities will get you into difficulties one of these days.

(Discreet tap on the door)

Come in.

(Discreet tap on the door)

RICHTER. (Louder) Come in, Herr Gombrich.

(GOMBRICH limps in. He is a very powerful looking individual. But for his limp he would have a stiff, correct, soldierly bearing)

GOMBRICH. Good news, sir, very good news indeed.

RICHTER. Well, let us hear what it is then, my dear fellow.

GOMBRICH. (Very formal, tries to straighten up) Leader Richter, the West Prescinct has declared for the National Health Party.

RICHTER. (Smacks his fist on the table) By God, we'll do it, then. That's two prescincts gone to us. One more and we march to the town hall. (Relaxes) Well, Gombrich, that is very good news. You will not be forgotten in the days of triumph. There'll be a place for you, my twisted old ally, you can depend upon that.

GOMBRICH. (Eagerly) Ah, Martin, I never thought...

RICHTER. What, old friend?

GOMBRICH. God bless you, Leader Richter. God bless the National Health Party.

RICHTER. Well, well. Go along. Let me hear as soon as more news comes in.

GOMBRICH. At once, Martin. At once, leader Richter.

(He limps out. There is a buzz of voices, typewriters and so on when the door opens)

HANS. That is very good. At the very worst we have voting parity with the Free Action Party. It seems as if the people are not responding to their dirty tricks.

RICHTER. (Striding up and down) Parity is not good enough. The second house is packed with hereditary Free Action agents. We need more than parity. If we can get the North Prescinct we can suspend the second chamber, declare an emergency and rule by fiat. After that...

(He spreads his hands out)

HANS. Farewell the Free Action Party.

RICHTER. Never assert the obvious. In any case we are a democratic party. We have no wish to impose an arbitrary sovereign will upon the community. What, my dear Hans, is our dominant slogan?

HANS. (Laughs) Well...

RICHTER. (Turns. Shouts) Mueller, what is our dominant slogan?

HANS. (Stiffens, stands up) Your pardon, Leader Richter, our dominant slogan is that in the political sphere the first person present indicative does not exist.

RICHTER. Schoolmaster. I need your brains, Hans, God knows, but you're a remote fellow. Not my will, but our will, say the people. That is our slogan. How can anyone say we are not a democratic party? Each voice of the party is the voice of the party and the voice of the party is the voice of the people.

HANS. Herr Richter?

(He comes from behind the desk. Leans on the side)

RICHTER. (Musing) Ten years. That's a long time.

HANS. Herr Richter?

RICHTER. Ten years of constant political activity,
constant frustration, constant peril. A lifetime of
dedication. I have destroyed myself in order to discover
the true soul of the people, my dear, subjective self,
my erring, individual, peculiar, wayward self. And
when I did that, only when I did that, was it clear to me
what it was that all men, because of their common
humanity, wanted and desired.

HANS. No-one but you could have done it.

RICHTER. No-one but me. No, perhaps not. Not alone,
anyway. Hans, my friend, I was born with a great love
of people and of all sentient things.

HANS. Yes.

RICHTER. Whatever moved and breathed. I had a great
delight in creation. In all its devious, changing change-
lessness. I was particularly addicted to observing the
apparently aimless and beautiful actions of fish.

HANS. Fish, Herr Richter?

RICHTER. Yes, Hans, fish. It sounds foolish but I used to
spend hours as a ragged child sitting on the bank of the
quiet stream that bordered our cottage, my head cupped
in my hands, watching the ways the fish, great and
small, aimless and sinuous, random, without meaning,
meandered and twisted. I took a deep pleasure in their
existence. At that time I took great delight in the idea
that each living thing was like nothing so much as itself.
And when I looked at my family and the families of
friends around me I was made sad by the fact that their
blessed uniqueness was distorted and damaged by the
laws of society.

HANS. That would be anarchy, Herr Richter.

(RICHTER walks up and down)

RICHTER. Mankind, I thought, is doomed by his necessity. He must murder himself in order to survive. But what survives, a broken creature, shuffling in herds from place to place, from hour to hour. And then it happened.

HANS. The moment of illumination to which you have often referred.

RICHTER. A moment such as the saints of the dead religions have spoken of. Seated one day by the little river and staring down into the water it suddenly seemed to me that far from it being the case that I could not say of the fish, now they will do this, now they will do that, I could discern, suddenly, a deep and underlying structure of action, each accepting or resisting the flow and eddy of water as a need common to each dictated. Suddenly the scales fell from my eyes. I watched, with deep joy, the slow and majestic dance of creation. I stood up and raised my hands to heaven. I turned back to the cottage. I looked at the face of my father, ruined with age and struggle. I said to myself: This must not be.

HANS. It was then...

RICHTER. I knew at once what I must do. No longer would men be driven into false shapes of order, laws devised by ignorant individualists. The law must proceed from the depths of our common humanity. The law must be the outward and visible expression of all that makes men men. At that moment occurred my terrible resolve, to destroy my false singularity, to discover the deep, organic principles of my being, to become the first truly universal man.

(His voice has risen to this last sentence)

Once that was achieved the patterns of human health and sickness were made clear to me. I was the living experiment and proof of the common desires of humanity. My will and the will of all men were given an objective identification, my will...

(The door bursts open)

RICHTER. (Irritably) What is this? What is this?

GOMBRICH. Herr Richter. Great news, great news.

(RICHTER steps forward)

RICHTER. How can you govern others if you cannot control yourselves? See that it does not happen again. Sick human material. Are you the ones upon which the burden of our efforts are to fall? You are like children. Well, well. What is your news?

GOMBRICH. Forgive us, Martin. You are quite right. We were being subjective. The news, Leader Richter, is good. Both the North and East Prescincts have declared for the National Health Party. The victory is complete.

RICHTER. (Quietly) The people have spoken. Where is Hemmel?

HEMMEL. Here, Leader Richter.

(HEMMEL is small and dark. He wears glasses)

RICHTER. Is everything ready?

HEMMEL. Everything is ready, Leader.

RICHTER. Get everyone in position. In two hours the complete re-organisation of the community must have taken place. I shall proceed directly to the Town Hall. Gümmel must be found and brought to me there. You will see to that, Hemmel.

HEMMEL. Right away, Leader Richter.

RICHTER. Now I should like you to leave me alone for a moment. Even you Hans. For possibly the last time in life I would like to be alone.

HANS. Certainly, Herr Richter. Leader Richter wishes to be alone.

GOMBRICH. Victory is ours, Martin.

RICHTER. The first victory of humanity, old friend. Off you go now. We must all be strong.

GOMBRICH. You are strong, leader. Our strength is yours.

RICHTER. Yes, yes. All leave me now, please.

(They go out. They turn and each bows and says: 'Leader Richter'. The door closes. RICHTER stands. Then he suddenly bursts out laughing. He begins to march around the room saying 'Leader Richter, Leader Richter'. He picks up an ash-tray and hurls it across the room. Then he begins to smash up the room. He jumps up on the desk. He shouts - 'Leader Richter'. He stops. Gets down. Sits in the seat behind the desk. Stares ahead of him)

RICHTER. When Gümmel is dead I don't know what I shall do.

(Enter MARIE. A pretty serving wench in her late twenties. She looks around)

MARIE. Well I never. Really, Herr Richter, you've gone too far this time. What a mess. What do you think Herr Gümmel will have to say?

RICHTER. It was an accident. I shall say it was an accident.

MARIE. And where are the others? Outside, I suppose, with the master's tape-recorder. The time and trouble you go to, all for that silly game of yours. Men of your age. I shall never understand it.

RICHTER. It's because... oh... you'll never understand.

MARIE. I don't suppose I will.

(Enter HANS, GOMBRICH and HEMMEL)

GOMBRICH. Were we good this time, Martin?

RICHTER. Very good. How was my speech, Hans?

HANS. Extremely formidable. Very eloquent. I liked the changes. My early years... that bit. Very effective.

GOMBRICH. You've made a right mess of this room, Martin.

MARIE. Well, you lot shouldn't encourage him.

HEMMEL. Marie, my love. Let me pinch your posterior.

GOMBRICH. We all hate Gümmel, Marie. We've all good reason to do so.

MARIE. Keep your fingers to yourself. When I want your attentions I'll ask for them.

HANS. Quite right. Let me nibble your ears. Let me rub noses like an oily Eskimo.

RICHTER. We'll have to get this place tidied up. He'll be back anytime now.

MARIE. Hans, if you weren't so horrible you'd be quite nice.

HANS. And vice-versa I'm sure. Will you marry me, Marie?

GOMBRICH. Careful, Hans. If Gümmel catches you you know what will happen.

RICHTER. Curse and damn Gümmel. I'd like to tear him limb from limb.

MARIE. Herr Gümmel is a good and very kind and studious gentleman. You have no reason to hate him. No reason at all.

(Door slams)

RICHTER. Good God, he's here. Come on, come on. Get this place tidied up. Oh, God, Marie. Go and distract him.

(Door opens)

GÜMMEL. Marie. Are you... Good God. What in God's name have you all been up to.

RICHTER. I can explain, Herr Gümmel.

GÜMMEL. What's this ash-tray doing over here?

RICHTER. I can explain all that, Herr Gümmel.

GÜMMEL. You are a seasoned and prolific liar, Richter. Can you explain it, Gombrich?

GOMBRICH. The facts... are...

GÜMMEL. Can you explain, Mueller, how my desk appears to have been attacked by a squadron of sledge-hammers? How my beautiful portrait is lying face down, on the floor, eh, Mueller, you animal?

MUELLER. It is all very regrettable, sir.

GÜMMEL. Regrettable. It's regrettable, is it? And who regrets it, eh? Is it your desk? Your ash-tray? Your portrait?

RICHTER. Herr Gümmel.

GÜMMEL. (Bellowing) Well, Richter, you liar? Well?

RICHTER. It was a quarrel, sir. A fight.

HANS. That's it, Herr Gümmel. There was a fight.

GOMBRICH. It was awful, Herr Gümmel.

RICHTER. Pardon me, Gombrich. You don't know the full facts.

GÜMMEL. I'm sure he doesn't. Nobody knows what the liar is going to say next.

RICHTER. This is the plain, blunt truth, Herr Gümmel.

You see, it was about Marie.

MARIE. Really!

GÜMMEL. What about Marie?

RICHTER. Well, Herr Gümmel, you see, Hans is very taken with Marie.

HANS. Martin!

RICHTER. It has to come out, Hans. The master must know the truth.

GOMBRICH. Yes, it's better to bring it all into the open.

RICHTER. Well, Herr Mueller told me today that Marie... I'm sorry Marie... Marie was... er... is... well... pregnant.

GÜMMEL. What! What's that?

MARIE. Herr Gümmel. This is all nonsense.

GÜMMEL. Is it? Is it? Nonsense, is it? You're all such a set of lying wretches I don't know whom to trust. I'm going to get to the bottom of this. Who, Richter, is the father of the child? Is it him, that young lecher, that Mueller? Mueller, is it you?

MUELLER. Er...

(He looks at RICHTER)

RICHTER. No, it is not. The father of the child is... Hemmel.

HEMMEL. Richter.

RICHTER. For God's sake don't deny it, Hemmel. You see, Herr Gümmel, that boy worships the ground she treads on and when he heard what had been going on he could not control himself. They came in here to speak to me about it and before you could say Jack Robinson they were at each other's throats.

GÜMMEL. Is that true, Mueller?

MUELLER. I'm sorry, sir. Yes, it's true. I saw red.

GÜMMEL. Hemmel?

HEMMEL. (Reluctantly, staring at RICHTER) It is true,
    Herr Gümmel.

GÜMMEL. Well, Marie.

MARIE. It's all lies, Herr Gümmel. Him. I wouldn't be
    seen dead with him. That nasty old thing. Ugh. I'll tell
    you what happened.

GÜMMEL. I don't wish to hear it. It's disgusting. You, of
    all people.

MARIE. But he just made it up, Herr Gümmel. He just
    made it up to cover his tracks. It's because of the silly
    game they play.

GÜMMEL. Game? What game?

RICHTER. Marie, please.

MARIE. Don't 'please' me, Richter, you horrible twisted
    creature. Fancy saying I'm pregnant. Look, Herr
    Gümmel. I'll go next door and bring in the tape-recorder.

RICHTER. You'll live to regret this, Marie.

GÜMMEL. Silence, Richter. I mean to get to the bottom of
    this. Go and fetch the tape-recorder, Marie.

MARIE. Right away, Herr Gümmel.

HANS. It's all up with us now, Martin.

RICHTER. That stupid girl. It's all her fault.

HEMMEL. I was a reluctant party. Please understand that,

93

Herr Gümmel. I was only obeying orders.

GÜMMEL. Orders? Whose orders?

RICHTER. Hemmel. You traitor.

HANS. We were just obeying Leader Richter, Herr Gümmel.

GOMBRICH. We were simply doing our duty.

GÜMMEL. Leader Richter. Leader Richter. What are you all talking about? What sort of madness is this?

(Enter MARIE)

What's all this, Marie? What does it mean?

MARIE. Listen to this, Herr Gümmel.

(She switches on the tape-recorder. Sound of type-writers, people, etc.)

MARIE. No, a bit later on.

(She switches it on a bit)

MANY VOICES. (On tape-recorder) Leader Richter, Leader Richter.

GÜMMEL. Good God!

(Tape continues, RICHTER speaking)

RICHTER. (On tape) People, men and women, old and young, the nightmare of mankind is over, the dark age is ended. We have opened our eyes and we look into the light.

VOICES. Leader Richter, Leader Richter.

RICHTER. (On tape) The days of care and sadness are over, the sick fever is past, the days of joy and health are all to be. The traitor Gümmel...

94

(At these words there is a roar as from a crowd)

GÜMMEL. What's that?

RICHTER. (On tape) ... the traitor Gümmel has been eliminated. The stain of his blood has cleansed our land. Men and women, people of this country, let us dedicate...

(GÜMMEL switches it off)

GÜMMEL. Well. Now what about that? What have you been up to, Richter?

RICHTER. (Sharply) Stand up.

(HANS, GOMBRICH and HEMMEL spring to attention)

Seize the criminal Gümmel.

GÜMMEL. God help us, the poor man is deranged.

HEMMEL. Is this wise?

RICHTER. No questions. Obey the order. See that he is held safe and secure until we decide what is to be done.

HANS. Right, leader. Come along, Gümmel.

GÜMMEL. You'll all go to gaol for this. Richter, I'll see you in a mental institution.

MARIE. Hans, what are you doing?

RICHTER. No more talk. There's been too much talk. Take him away.

(They drag GÜMMEL out shouting - 'Let me alone. I'm the Master here')

MARIE. You've gone too far this time, Richter.

RICHTER. The die is cast, Marie. The die is cast.

(End of scene. A song is heard: 'Weisst Du Wieviel Sternlein Stehen'. All the music, except the 'Horst Wessel' song, is taken from 'A Treasury of German Folk Song', sung by the Vienna Radio Choir. As the song begins RICHTER and MARIE look up, listen and smile. The song continues as the curtain closes and is still playing when it opens.)

SCENE TWO

(RICHTER listens a moment and then goes back to
speaking into the phone. He is seated at the desk. The
scene is the same room. Now the portrait of GUMMEL
is gone.)

RICHTER. No, madam. I'm afraid the master is not at
home. What? Yes. Certainly, as soon as he returns.
No, Madam. Sometime next week, I think. Well... I
couldn't say. Urgent business, he said. Thank you,
Madam. Goodbye.

(Enter MARIE with tea-tray)

MARIE. Who was that?

RICHTER. His sister. Put it there.

MARIE. I must be crazy going on like this.

RICHTER. You like Hans, don't you?

MARIE. I suppose so.

RICHTER. Well, then. What happens to the child if he goes
to prison?

MARIE. You will make him marry me, won't you? Now I
really am pregnant.

RICHTER. We'll see, we'll see. Have they finished out
there?

MARIE. I want to say that what you're doing is cruel and

horrible. Hans told me something of your past and I suppose being a servant is something of a come-down but all the same, things are changed now. It's not your lot in control now. We're finished with all that.

RICHTER. Hold your tongue. You're a silly girl. Have they finished out there yet?

MARIE. Yes. Hans says they're going to bring it in here.

RICHTER. Good. Tell him to fetch it now.

MARIE. I wish I'd never come to this place.

RICHTER. Miaow. Tell Hans to bring it in.

(Knock at the door)

Come.

GOMBRICH. It's ready, Leader.

RICHTER. Good; bring it in.

(HANS, GOMBRICH and HEMMEL begin to drag in the four separate sides of a large wooden cage. They staple each side to the floor, at one side of the room. HEMMEL beings in the top of the cage. He slides the roof on. It slots into one of the sides and padlocks on the other. For the moment it is not locked)

A very fine job, Hemmel, you are to be congratulated. Very beautiful. A giant rat cage for a giant rat. Is it strong? Is it secure?

HEMMEL. Only a superman could get out of that, leader.

RICHTER. Ha, ha. A good joke, Hemmel. Gümmel is no superman. Where is he?

HANS. He's next door, tied up. Shall I fetch him?

RICHTER. Do that.

(HANS goes out)

RICHTER. Lovely craftsmanship, Hemmel. You are a genius.

HEMMEL. A cage like that will last a life-time.

GOMBRICH. (Slaps HEMMEL on the back) Our Hemmel is in good form today, Leader.

RICHTER. Why shouldn't he be, old Gombrich? He's made the leap from freedom into necessity. Order has come again. Hemmel knows what to do. Right, Hemmel?

HEMMEL. Right, Leader. I've got no complaints.

RICHTER. Well, there's not many can say as much. Ah!

(Enter HANS with GÜMMEL. GÜMMEL is bound at the wrists, has a blindfold on and his mouth is taped. He stands dejected and helpless)

RICHTER. Ah! The mighty midget, Gümmel. Lord rat himself.

(He turns GÜMMEL round and round. He stops and GUMMEL stumbles)

Remove the rope, Hans.

(HANS does so)

And the blindfold. No, on second thoughts. Yes. Yes. Remove the blindfold. There. Gümmel redivivus. Hail, Gümmel. Now, all of you. Look on the great Gümmel.

HANS. Hail Gümmel.

MARIE. I'm going.

HANS. Marie. Marie.

RICHTER. Let her go, Hans. She won't go far.

HANS. That girl needs a lesson.

RICHTER. Well, Gombrich. Well, Hemmel. Aren't you going to make your obeisances?

GOMBRICH. Of course, Leader. Hail, Gümmel.

HEMMEL. Hail Gümmel.

RICHTER. Put the great Gümmel into his cage.

(They lift him up and drop him in. He crawls around and then stands up, gripping the bars)

RICHTER. Grrrr, Gümmel. What do you think of your nice, new cage, eh?

GOMBRICH. He likes it, leader.

RICHTER. Of course he does. Alright, now, off you go, all of you. Enjoy yourselves. Report to me this evening. We've a lot to decide.

GOMBRICH. Right, Leader Richter.

HEMMEL. Tonight, Leader.

RICHTER. That's right. That's right.

(They exit)

RICHTER. Well, Herr Gümmel, if you won't bite me I'll take that stuff off your mouth. Will you bite me, sir?

(GÜMMEL shakes his head)

Alright, I trust you. There. Did it hurt?

(They speak to one another in a very genial fashion)

GÜMMEL. No. It did not.

RICHTER. Good. I'm not a cruel man, Herr Gümmel. I sent the others away so we could have a talk. Would you like some tea?

GÜMMEL. Thank you, Richter.

RICHTER. Just you make yourself comfortable and I'll give
you your tea.

GÜMMEL. How are you going to get yourself out of this
mess, Richter?

RICHTER. God alone knows that, Herr Gümmel. God alone
knows.

GÜMMEL. You'll have to let me go, Richter.

(They enjoy their tea throughout this humane discussion
and behave in a very civilised way)

RICHTER. If I let you go, Herr Gümmel...

GÜMMEL. Call me Franz, Richter, now you're a man of
authority. And I'll call you Martin.

RICHTER. Would that be proper?

GÜMMEL. How punctilious you are. I should say... yes...
the balance of power - despite appearances - is evenly
distributed. I don't have the power to let myself out and
you can't keep me in. As things stand I should say it
would be quite proper to be on first name terms.

RICHTER. Very well, Franz. Why do you think I have to
let you go?

GÜMMEL. Because you're a sensible man, Martin. There
are bound to be enquiries. A man in my position is
needed for something every day. I have many friends,
enemies, associates, competitors. Sooner than later
they'll all be making enquiries and sooner than later
they're bound to come here.

RICHTER. What will happen, Franz, if I do let you out?

GÜMMEL. Within half an hour you'll all be behind bars

yourselves. The others, well, you know about the
others...

RICHTER. Well, for Hemmel and Gombrich, I suppose it's
life. For Hans, well, he was only a boy. He hardly had
time to commit a real atrocity.

GÜMMEL. True. But when these recent events are known,
Martin, well... there are political implications...
political implications.

RICHTER. Ah, there it is, then. I must say you're being
very frank with me, Herr Gümmel.

GÜMMEL. There's no point in being otherwise, Martin.
You know as well as I do I could never let this pass. It
flies in the face of order, it's a blow against the whole
fabric of society, besides being a direct insult to me.
What surprises me, Martin, is how you got yourself
mixed up in an absurdity of this sort.

RICHTER. Partly your fault, Franz. In a way, you have
only yourself to blame. You remember, after the
collapse you told me you saw your way to getting some
very good staff. You remember, Franz?

GÜMMEL. I do remember, Martin. When I found my way
to getting hold of those party members... everybody
was doing it... after all they are our people... and
taking them on I knew I would be getting good and faithful servants and doing my bit for old causes at the same
time.

RICHTER. Well, Franz, while I understood your sentiments
and again, Franz, while I fully understood that they
were bound to your obedience by the knowledge you had
of them...

GÜMMEL. Knowledge indeed. Hemmel... he'd be lucky to
get away with a life sentence...

RICHTER. While I understood all this I knew as soon as I
saw their faces what would happen.

GÜMMEL. Nothing happened. They've been excellent servants. I couldn't have hoped for a better odd-job man than Hemmel. And Gombrich has turned out to be an excellent gardener-cum-chauffeur.

RICHTER. From your point of view, yes, Franz, but did you ever think of my position. I was, as you know, apolitical. As your butler I have always considered it enough if my work was found satisfactory and I never heard that you had any cause to complain.

GÜMMEL. My dear Martin. Your conduct has always been exemplary.

RICHTER. Thank you for that. I used to see on my gravestone the words, service, dedication, a good servant. Well, all that was rudely shattered when they came stamping into the house.

GÜMMEL. Ah, I see.

RICHTER. You see now, Franz, when it's too late. At first they ignored me. Then it turned to open contempt. Of course they never mentioned the old days but they were always at it with sly innuendoes. That girl, Marie, took up with Mueller and soon I couldn't get a civil word out of her. I was less than the dirt.

GÜMMEL. My poor Martin. I never knew.

RICHTER. Why should you? I never complained. But many's the night I lay on my bed and cursed you and the day you brought them here.

GÜMMEL. I quite understand.

RICHTER. I wonder if you do, Franz. All your life you've been used to position, power, authority. A man dies without some authority, unless he's a cripple, a slave, an homunculus.

GÜMMEL. An homunculus, Martin!

RICHTER. You may laugh, Franz. To me it's no joke. The

103

only power I ever had was here; in this house. I found my manhood here and it was here I almost lost it.

GUMMEL. Ah.

RICHTER. I told them lies, Franz. I told them I knew what they were because I recognised them from old photographs at headquarters. I told them I had kept quiet until I was sure they would not betray me. I told them I was a very important figure at H.Q. and soon we were talking about the old days. I was inspired, Franz. I told them that a new programme was emerging from the wreck of the old. I became the prophet of the new movement. I used to lie awake at night inventing new slogans. We acted the day we would march into power again. We gave a name to those who stood between us and authority. We called that impediment...

GUMMEL. Gummel. I see. I see. But Martin. You're a Swebian.

RICHTER. (Very agitated) Don't say that. Not even when we're alone.

GUMMEL. But you are, you are. I protected you. One word from me and you'd have been little flakes of ash fluttering on the wind. I kept it dark. You're a pure Swebian; if there can be such a thing.

RICHTER. Yes, I'm a Swebian. But what I told them was that you were a Swebian.

GUMMEL. Richter. I'm angry. An old family like mine. Now, for the first time, I'm really angry.

RICHTER. I showed them the depth of their degradation. They were servants, bound to the service of a Swebian. From that moment they were mine.

GUMMEL. Not for long, Martin. One word from me and they'll cut your throat from ear to ear.

RICHTER. I think not, Gummel, I think not. They would only regard it as another Swebian lie.

GÜMMEL. Look, Martin. Open this cage. Let me go.
Every minute I stay here things get worse and worse.
Let me go now and I'll see things don't get too hard for
you. I can't guarantee anything, of course, but I'll do
my best. For old time's sake.

RICHTER. But you don't understand, Franz. I'm not afraid
of the consequences. You don't understand. I am the
leader. They believe in me. They do what I say. I am
the common man. I can save the country.

GÜMMEL. Don't be absurd. Stop playing games. Open this
cage door.

(He begins to walk round the cage)

RICHTER. Open the door. No. Goodbye to you, Franz.
Goodbye to you, Herr Gümmel. My first political act
will be to remove this Swebish filth from this house. If
the house is dirty we clean the house. If the body is
diseased we kill the disease. Or it kills us. All life is
a form of killing. We kill to live. We kill to move. The
plants die under our feet, the birds drop from the trees.
What are you but a living cancer? The cancer we must
root out, eliminate, cancer, choking, filthy cancer.

GÜMMEL. Stop it, stop it. Come back to your senses.
Those days are done with. We live in different times.

RICHTER. The times have changed but the needs are the
same. Do you know, Swebish man, when I first realised
the deep eternal truths lurking in the obscure, swirling
depths of political reality? I was a small, ragged boy...

GÜMMEL. Martin. Martin. Listen. Listen.

RICHTER. As I watched I seemed to see, beneath all that
beautiful disorder, the dance of creation, beneath the
disorder, a strange and mystic harmony, flowing and
dancing, tides of reality, the fish swayed,

(He moves round the cage)

the fish swayed, flowing and swaying with the tides of

their needs. I saw my old father... my old Swebish
man... my own father...

GÜMMEL. Let me out. Let me out. You damned lunatic.
Let me out.

(RICHTER stands stock-still)

RICHTER. Dead. He's dead. Crushed like an egg. Their
boots... whose boots... THEIR boots. It's not
natural...

GÜMMEL. Please...

RICHTER. Ruined. Smashed. Smashed...

(He shouts at GÜMMEL)

You damned Swebish man.

SCENE THREE

(Scene: The garden. Very pleasant. HANS and MARIE are sitting on a small green mound. HANS is chewing grass. Song: 'Am Brunnen Vor Dem Tore'.)

HANS. It's very peaceful. I like this garden, Marie. I really do.

MARIE. Yes, it's nice. I wish...

HANS. Hush, Marie. Don't think of anything. Just relax with nature.

MARIE. Hans, what?

HANS. No questions, Marie. Let it go. (He looks around) Very peaceful. (He hums the song) When I was a boy, Marie, we used to go for long walks in the woods. Very early when the moon was hardly gone, when the sun was just about to appear. We heard the dawn chorus. I liked that very much.

MARIE. At home, Hans, we have some very nice woods too. When I was a little girl we used to go for picnics in the woods. Me and my brothers and sisters and my father and my mother. We used to run away and hide and then pretend we were lost and cry out for mother or father and they would call back and then we would run and run until we found them again.

HANS. We ought to go for a picnic one day, Marie. We really ought to do that.

MARIE. Hans?

HANS. You're going into an interrogative mood. I told you. It spoils everything.

MARIE. What is going to happen... now... Hans?

HANS. You heard the leader, Marie. He gave us a new slogan. It hit me like a ton of bricks.

MARIE. Hans. You're an intelligent boy. You used to be a schoolteacher. I heard Herr Richter say so...

HANS. It's a joke of his. Because I was at university. But listen, Marie.

(A deep groan is heard)

MARIE. Oh, I can't bear it. It's terrible.

(A deep groan)

What are they doing?

HANS. It's Hemmel. He's practising.

MARIE. He's what?

HANS. Forget it. I was saying, Marie, the leader gave us a new slogan.

MARIE. New rubbish.

HANS. Marie, don't say that. You mustn't ever talk like that.

MARIE. Hans, do you love me?

HANS. He said 'Swebish is as Swebish does'. That's where we made our mistake before, Marie. Now, thank Richter, we know better.

MARIE. Hans, dear. Dear, Hans.

HANS. You're not listening.

MARIE. Yes, I was. You were saying, 'Marie, I don't love you.'

HANS. How silly you are. I love you... er...

MARIE. How much?

HANS. More than somewhat.

MARIE. How much is that?

HANS. When the child is born he'll be the first born in the century of the new order.

MARIE. Oh, Hans. It's terrible. When the police come they'll take you away and they'll hang you. And our baby will be born and where will he look for his father.

HANS. If they hang me I'll be dancing up in the air. Tell him to look up. And there I'll be.

MARIE. Hans. Please. What will happen?

(Long groan)

I can't bear it. (She puts her hands to her ears; runs off)

(HANS pursues her)

HANS. Marie. Marie. (Stops) Squeamish girl. Woman. She ought to know. Pain is necessary. That's what Leader Richter says. She ought to know that.

(Enter RICHTER)

RICHTER. What ought who to know, Hans?

HANS. Marie. She can't bear the sound of Hemmel practising on Herr Gümmel.

(Long groan)

RICHTER. It is rather distracting. But necessary.

(Long groan)

RICHTER. We must habituate ourselves to the sound of essential pain.

(Long groan)

Damn that noise. (He shouts) Hemmel.

HEMMEL. (Off) Leader Richter?

RICHTER. Switch that damn thing off, will you? That's enough for this morning.

HEMMEL. (Comes on with the tape-recorder. It groans. He switches it off) It's off, Leader Richter.

RICHTER. Good. It's very odd how difficult it is to ignore it. I can understand Marie's feelings.

HANS. You, Leader Richter?

RICHTER. Yes, Hans. Are you surprised?

HANS. I'm a bit confused. For one thing, didn't you say that Hemmel was practising on Herr Gümmel?

RICHTER. Yes. I remember very distinctly saying that.

HANS. Well, he wasn't. It was the tape-recorder.

RICHTER. Of course, Hans. What d'you expect? One thing you have to learn, my boy, is to believe everything you are ordered to believe. Complete trust, you understand. And when, for whatever reason, you find out that it was wrong, well, you accept the necessity for the lie.

HEMMEL. He's young, Leader Richter.

RICHTER. But willing, Hemmel. Very willing. You see, Hans, if I think you ought to get used to the idea of pain and if I don't want a hair of Herr Gümmel's head touched, for whatever reason, I have to tell you a lie. It's the only way to achieve the end we all agree to be desirable. Truth cannot be more important than the end it serves, and the end it serves is the good of the people.

HANS. Of course, Herr Richter. I am stupid.

RICHTER. On the contrary, Hans. You are highly intelligent.

HANS. I hope I am, Herr Richter, for the party's sake. But one more thing troubles me. I...

RICHTER. Well, my boy?

HANS. I hardly like to...

HEMMEL. Out with it, Mueller. By God, I hate any kind of womanish sentimentality.

RICHTER. You are a wolf and a dunderhead, Hemmel. That is what you are. You are hands and feet, Hemmel, and your tongue is for saying 'yes' with.

HEMMEL. Yes, Leader Richter.

RICHTER. I know what is troubling you, Hans. You noticed how disturbed I was by the sound of that groaning. You noticed that I found it difficult to fix my mind on anything, that I was, how shall I say, always waiting for the next groan.

HANS. That is right, Leader Richter. It occurred to me, at H.Q. Leader Richter must have been hearing groans all the time. At H.Q. there must have been groans from morning till night.

RICHTER. Good God. How innocent you are. The existence of pain has to be justified, Hans. It is perfectly natural and proper to wish to abolish it. Do you think we should all develop the same functional propensities as an executioner, a surgeon or a Hemmel? Of course not. They are necessary, not to cause pain, but to cause that pain which leads to the greater good of the people. Some people cannot bear the shriek of a pig. Or the

111

squeal of a rabbit. They are good people. When there is pain they gather round to remove it. But they are also sensible people. It doesn't stop them from enjoying roast pork or a rabbit stew. If everybody were as inured to pain as Hemmel we'd claw each other to pieces. If everybody was as sensitive as Marie we'd all die of compassion. The leader is a man whose thought recognises the necessity of pain, whose humanity hates the sound of it.

HANS. I see.

RICHTER. The butchers need to lose their humanity. All my test was designed to discover was who was a natural butcher and who was not.

HANS. How do I come out, Leader Richter?

RICHTER. Well, Hans, it's early days yet. We shall see.

(Enter GOMBRICH, very agitated)

GOMBRICH. Leader Richter. Come at once.

RICHTER. What is it, old friend?

GOMBRICH. It's Herr Gümmel. He's been taken with a sort of seizure.

RICHTER. Good. Good. Does it look serious?

GOMBRICH. Very serious.

(A deep groan is heard then a gasp. Enter MARIE)

MARIE. Oh Hans, the poor old man.

HANS. Pull yourself together, Marie. Tell us what happened.

RICHTER. A butcher. It begins to look like it. All of you, listen. This is a fortunate happening. Obviously Herr Gümmel is on his last legs. It would be a kindness to expedite his passing. I want you all to stay here. When

I return, everything will be finished for him.

ALL. Leader Richter.

MARIE. Hans. Herr Gombrich. What are you saying?

(Exit RICHTER)

HANS. Silence, Marie. One more word out of you and I can see that Leader Richter will begin to think you are not worthy to be a new mother. Then God knows what will happen.

MARIE. What... oh.

(In the meantime HEMMEL has been fiddling with his little black box. At MARIE's 'ah' a deep groan comes from the box)

GOMBRICH. What are you doing, Hemmel?

HEMMEL. One moment, Gombrich, please. Ah.

(Music to drown the groans pours forth, the theme from Tannhauser or the Guten abend, Gut' nacht song)

There. Do you not feel your soul stirring when you hear this music, Gombrich?

GOMBRICH. I think it exactly expresses the spirit of our people, Hemmel. That is my opinion.

HEMMEL. (Hums the tune) You are right. Yes, you are right.

HANS. It is very beautiful. Don't you think so, Marie?

(Enter RICHTER)

MARIE. What did you say, Hans?

HANS. Herr Hemmel's music. It is very beautiful.

MARIE. I suppose so.

RICHTER. (Quietly) A heart attack. Poor Herr Gümmel.
It was a merciful release.

GOMBRICH. We salute your integrity, Leader Richter.

ALL. We salute your integrity, Leader Richter.

(The scene ends on a musical crescendo from
HEMMEL's tape-recorder.)

SCENE FOUR

(A large dining room. A dinner, very lavish it is too, HERREN RICHTER, GOMBRICH, HEMMEL and MUELLER. MARIE is serving)

RICHTER. No, no, Hemmel, that was before, surely, before the second putsch.

HEMMEL. I don't want to argue with you, Leader. You were there, I wasn't.

RICHTER. I think you'll find my memory serves me right. It's hardly likely I'd forget an occasion like that. Marie.

MARIE. (Dully) Coming.

RICHTER. More wine, Marie. Let's have more of the despicable Gümmel's choice wine.

(She goes out. Returns. Pours out wine)

See to your beloved Hans, Marie. He'll make a fine butcher one day, eh Hans?

HANS. Whatever you say, Leader.

RICHTER. That's right. That's right. Whatever I say. You listen to what I say, Hans. I feel like a father to you, my boy. I really do.

GOMBRICH. You're in good spirits tonight, Martin.

RICHTER. Good spirits. Splendid spirits. I know, friends, (He staggers to his feet) I know that all over our country today there are men and women like us waiting and hoping for a new dawn, a return to life, a lifting up of the bowed head of the people, of the people's party. Gentlemen, brothers, I give you a toast...

(They all rise)

To the people.

ALL. To the people.

RICHTER. Vigour, hope and power to the National Health Party.

ALL. The National Health Party.

GOMBRICH. Herr Leader.

RICHTER. Herr Gombrich?

GOMBRICH. Might I ask?

RICHTER. Ask away.

GOMBRICH. What... was... the... what was... he ... like in the early days?

(Hush)

HEMMEL. Oh, God. Dead. Dead. Tell us, Herr Richter, tell us.

HANS. I never saw him, not in the flesh.

RICHTER. My friends, my good friends, how can I... like a rock, like a pillar of fire... not human... a god. Never weary, friends never, not once, disturbed, eyes blue as steel, commanding, certain, his mind a thunder cloud lit by flashes of lightning, an eagle, a lion, a natural king... he was... a natural king.

GOMBRICH. Exactly as I remembered him, Leader. Exactly. Though I only saw him at a distance.

RICHTER. Gombrich, you remember, when he appeared the air was different, he changed the air, old men were made strong, the sick, the crippled, they longed to jump and walk. The women - (He grins) you know - the fat blonde maidens, and the dark ones too for that matter, they worshipped him. You know half the babies that were born then were born by women who were vicariously giving themselves to the leader.

HANS. Did he... ?

RICHTER. Never. His will was like iron. Courteous, yes, considerate, yes. But... never.

HEMMEL. Wonderful. Wonderful.

RICHTER. More wine. More wine. Marie.

(She fills up their glasses)

He was a great man.

GOMBRICH. A great man. And it's a big piece of luck for us, Leader, to find someone as close to him as you were.

RICHTER. Right, Gombrich, right. But great as he was, he was not great enough.

GOMBRICH. What!

HEMMEL. What are you saying?

HANS. The leader. Him. I...

(He staggers to his feet)

RICHTER. Sit down. Be silent. I repeat, not great enough. He failed.

HEMMEL. He never failed. We failed. We failed.

RICHTER. You failed. Of course you failed. Why did you fail?

GOMBRICH. Because we were not as strong as he was.

RICHTER. Right, Gombrich. He failed because he expected everyone to share his strength and gradually even his strength was not enough, not for the collective power of the people. He was too large, too great, not great enough. Now, everything is changed.

HANS. How, Herr Richter?

RICHTER. Now everything I ask is possible. Everyone acts together, for each other, with each other. We are the point of the spear. The mass of the people will thrust it home. Everyone finds his place, everyone takes his place and the juggernaut of the state slowly... slowly... gentlemen... it creaks, it moves, it gathers pace, it gathers momentum, it leaps forward, it crushes the world to the true shape of its iron wheels. That is the way, gentlemen, the new way, the power of each is the power of all, the power of all is the power of each, one state, one people, one leader.

ALL. One state, one people, one leader.

RICHTER. The old words but to a new melody. Drink up. Drink up. Wine is blood. Drink, drink. The blood of the earth. The people will grow like wheat, golden acres of people, the blonde wheat will wave in the winds of the world. Drink up, drink up.

ALL. One state, one people, one leader.

RICHTER. Never too weak, never too slow. But on, on, on. The hills go down before us. The worlds tilt at our pleasure. We'll shoot the planets out of the sky, we'll dance and roar through space. Each man a god and every god his own universe. When the king is come and heaven's emperor opens the sky, unlocks the light and the angels. The dawn is the blood of morning. Acres of wheat, mountains of vines. Drink. Drink.

HEMMEL. God. I wish it would begin.

RICHTER. It has begun. It has begun. You old fool.

GOMBRICH. Good, good, Leader. I'm very happy tonight.
Marie. Bring the Leader some good brandy.

RICHTER. That's it, Gombrich, old warrior. Where is
that girl?

HANS. I'll go and see where she is.

HEMMEL. No, you don't, my lad. You stay here and drink
with the Leader. Keep your hands off the women for one
night.

HANS. I wasn't. I mean... Herr Richter, I wasn't.

RICHTER. Poor lad. You've embarrassed him, Hemmel.
He means well by the girl, you understand. Not like you,
eh, Gombrich? How many honest women have you met
in your time?

GOMBRICH. Never had much time or opportunity, Leader.
The sort of women that did for me were the sort to keep
you warm and kick you out. Strictly a business
transaction, money for pleasure. That's the only sort
of women I ever knew.

HEMMEL. You drunken old brute. You must have had a
mother.

GOMBRICH. My mother...

HEMMEL. Not another word. Mothers are sacred. You
understand.

RICHTER. Very well said, Hemmel. You had a good mother.

HEMMEL. A lovely mother, leader. I reverence her
memory. Gombrich, I order you to drink to the memory
of my beautiful mother.

GOMBRICH. You drunken swine. I'll snap you in two. Your
mother was a...

HEMMEL. Drink, Gombrich. Drink, you stupid animal.
Drink or I'll pluck the teeth from your mouth, I'll

scrape your bowels, I'll...

RICHTER. Silence, Hemmel. Gombrich, apologise to Hemmel.

GOMBRICH. That...

RICHTER. Gombrich. Apologise to Hemmel.

GOMBRICH. I apologise... to Hemmel.

RICHTER. Hemmel... accept the apology of Gombrich.

HEMMEL. I... accept... the apology... of Gombrich.

RICHTER. Good. That is good. This must not happen again. Marie.

MARIE. Yes.

RICHTER. Brandy for Gombrich. Brandy for Hemmel. Come. Good. Hemmel, Gombrich, drink to brotherhood Touch glasses. Drink.

GOMBRICH and HEMMEL. Brotherhood.

(They throw their glasses in the fire)

RICHTER. Hans, drink to brotherhood.

HANS. Brotherhood.

(Does likewise)

Will you drink to brotherhood, Leader?

RICHTER. Brotherhood... yes... (He looks in his glass, glances from one to the other) Brotherhood. (He turns and then deliberately smashes his glass in the fire) Well now, Gombrich, after all that, tell us something about the old days.

GOMBRICH. Me? No. Excuse me, Leader. I have no memories.

120

HEMMEL. Yes. Come along. Gombrich. Tell us about the old times.

GOMBRICH. What about them? They were good until the end. And then they were bad.

HANS. Tell us about the good times.

GOMBRICH. Well, what I remember best is one day...

RICHTER. That's it, go on, Gombrich.

GOMBRICH. One day, in December, the ground was like iron. We'd been moving forward by inches. They were like grey wolves, a sudden rush and then nothing, melted away in the darkness. We were not in good heart, tired, afraid, yes, afraid, but determined not to give ground. I knew if we didn't break them soon the winter would come down and we'd be broken. I watched the cold coming up over the sky, the snows gathering in the east, I could see our death spreading its grey snow wings in the darkness, I could, almost, see it.

HANS. That was terrible, Herr Gombrich.

GOMBRICH. It was, my boy, terrible. One more assault, I thought, before we're finished. I gave out the orders. I should say, Leader, we could see, sometimes, the lights of the town in the distance. We would almost hear voices, singing, almost smell the warmth and the life there. We sometimes heard bells. Some of the men thought that the worst of it, hearing the bells in the white, blank air and hearing, now and again, a gun fire or a rifle crack. Well...

HEMMEL. What did you do?

GOMBRICH. I decided on one more attack. (He rises; goes forward; begins to act it) I asked Headquarters for whatever support they could give me. At 0.500 hours we were all ready. We were all lying ready. Then, faintly at first, then louder and louder, like a swarm of gnats, of bees, of wasps, like a roar of demons, they came over, hundreds, it seemed, hundreds, ours,

121

fighters, bombers, down, down, down, screaming and
twisting, earth leaping into the sky, over and over...
and then we went in. On and on we went and back and
back they went, the earth boiling under their them and then,
looking up, we saw...

RICHTER. What? What?

GOMBRICH. The town, beautiful it was, like a roman
candle, the buildings were all moving and falling. We
roared into the town, the bombers swooped off. They
dipped their wings. The town was our own.

HANS. Well done, Gombrich.

HEMMEL. Tell us what happened next, Gombrich.

RICHTER. Let us hear the full, magnificent account
Gombrich, my friend.

GOMBRICH. What happened next... what happened next...
Leader Richter... I tell you... it was wonderful... you
see, Leader, our soldiers, the men, the officers, my
comrades, tired as they were, Leader, tired, wounded,
bleeding, their faces black with smoke, they... they
formed into ranks, everyone of them, wounded or not,
they formed up and marched past, saluting. I stood on
the steps, I saluted them and they saluted me... they
marched past... singing...

(He begins to sing the 'Horst Wessel' song, he is
weeping, he salutes. The others take up the song, they
sing it together. They stop. There is silence)

RICHTER. That night, outside the town, there was wailing
and lamentation. The wolves, the wolverines, the
Swebish swine... were howling.

GOMBRICH. (Coming to himself again) You heard that, did
you, Leader?

RICHTER. I heard the story. It was known to me.

HEMMEL. Gombrich, I must shake you by the hand. I am

122

proud to shake the hand of a hero of the people.

RICHTER. Salute to Gombrich.

ALL. Salute to Gombrich.

GOMBRICH. Thank you Leader. Thank you, brothers.

HEMMEL. This is excellent, excellent. Marie. Another bottle. Drink up, Leader. We will drink till our eyes are as red as blood.

RICHTER. Well said, Hemmel. You certainly know how to enjoy yourself.

HEMMEL. Of course, Leader, what is life without pleasure. A spartan monument, a cold cliff to hang on to, eh, Leader, a slippery track in a mountain of ice?

GOMBRICH. Hemmel is educated. Definitely educated. What d'you say to that, Hans, Do you have a capful of beautiful metaphors like Hemmel?

RICHTER. Leave the boy alone, Gombrich. He is shy. Aren't you, Hans?

HANS. Actions speak louder than words, Leader.

RICHTER. Good, good. That is right. When in doubt, act.

GOMBRICH. Hemmel should tell us something of the great days, Leader Richter. He has some good memories.

HEMMEL. That's so, Gombrich. I have some very good memories of those days, My mind is full of very good memories of that time, Leader.

RICHTER. Very well, Hemmel. Silence for Hemmel while he speaks of the old times.

HEMMEL. Gentlemen, Leader, we had a dream...

GOMBRICH. Right, Hemmel, right.

RICHTER. Shhh. Quiet. Tell us the dream.

HEMMEL. A dream. Yes, a very beautiful dream, a dream as clear and as pure as our skies, as strong as our forests, a dream as sublime as our mountains, a dream of purity, a dream of nobility, a dream of people like gods walking in a paradise of gardens.

(Song: - one verse -'Lang, Lang, ist's her'. They listen. They are moved)

RICHTER. Good, good. Very nice.

HEMMEL. But, Leader, as you know, like all dreams it contained its own darkness. A smirch, a foulness, a canker, a foul smelling thing, growing, spreading, a fever, a twisted malevolent power, walking and haunting our broad ways. I refer, brothers, to the grotesque and horrible phenomenon of Swebishness. Walk forward and a clinging wet hand caused you to stumble, think and a whispering voice distorted your thinking. Like a great tree, we were, besieged by crawling parasites. Action was called for. The knife must save the tree or the tree would die. I, Leader, was a small instrument of that cleansing. Day by day I saw the defaced statue of our country returning to its former magnificence.

HANS. Trees, statues, gardens. You are generous, Hemmel.

RICHTER. Go on, Hemmel. Forget our mimetic school-teacher.

HEMMEL. He doesn't understand, Leader, the great hopes, the dream, the nightmare, what had to be done. Terrible, terrible.

GOMBRICH. But you managed it, eh, Hemmel? You completed the task.

HEMMEL. I did my duty. Nothing impeded my duty. Some-times, Leader, inside, the sickness invaded me, a kind of weakness of nature. I... they almost confused us...

124

RICHTER. How do you mean, Hemmel?

HEMMEL. One day, Leader, I was walking by the banks of
a small river. I noticed one of them sitting by the bank,
an old one, an old man. He was sitting there, with his
head in his hands. He was looking at nothing. It was in
the very early days. I was a young man, learning my
way, fired with ideals, without the resolve to enact
them. I saw him, alone, quiet, dejected, by the bank of
the river. Old, worn, exhausted, dejected. A spring of
compassion... almost destroyed me. I knew this for a
moment of testing, a moment of crisis. I stood beside
him... his face turned up to me... he almost smiled.
Leader... that was the most treacherous moment of
my life. We looked at each other. In the way they have
he said, 'Well, friend?' I struggled, I put my hand to
my mouth, like this, Leader, I said 'you, you'. I
struck him, again, again and again. He crawled in front
of me. I struck down and down. He gave a kind of
stupid, stupid groan, that stupid old man, he groaned.
I said 'I'll stop your moaning. We'll have no more... of
... that.' I took my pistol. I cracked down at him. His
mouth spilled at my feet. Gombrich, Leader, I was
almost sick. Then he was quiet, a dirty, twisted, red
lump on the bank of our river. Leader, in that moment
I gloried. I lifted my head back and I laughed. I laughed.
I shouted, I danced. I said, looking at everything, the
river, the stones, the sky, I said - remember, I was
young - I said... 'you are all free, the monster is dead
... you are all free'. Free, free, free. (He stands,
fists clenched; he smiles) I was a fool, in those days,
Leader. I should have killed him, without hate, without
rancour, without feeling, as I would a bug. But I was
young. I thought I had earned my freedom.

RICHTER. It was the moaning, I suppose, Hemmel. The old
man moaning must have touched the tender tissues of
your young heart. Eh, Hemmel? Gombrich, give
Hemmel a drink. He relives his past. He is sweating.
It was the moaning. By a river. You did not notice,
Hemmel, what manner of fish there was in that river?

HEMMEL. Fish, Leader? I saw no fish.

RICHTER. There would be fish. No, Hemmel, you would not have noticed. A blood-soaked bank. You would not have noticed.

HEMMEL. I saw nothing like that, Leader.

RICHTER. Right. Right. He saw nothing. He saw nothing. Gombrich.

GOMBRICH. Are you well, Leader?

RICHTER. Well? No, I am dying. Of thirst, Gombrich. My glass is empty. I drink to your memory, Hemmel, to your mouth, your manhood, your courage, to kill an old man needs courage. Hemmel, my congratulations.

HEMMEL. I was a fool. It was nothing at all. Nothing. An old man. A bug. Nothing. Nothing.

RICHTER. Nothing at all. I drink to that. I drink to nothing at all. All of you, rise. Raise high your glasses. Drink now to a dead nothing, drink to nothing, drink to nothing at all.

HANS. I don't understand you, Leader.

RICHTER. Then don't understand. Do as I say. Do you need to understand everything? Gombrich, do you understand?

GOMBRICH. No, Leader.

HEMMEL. I understand, Leader.

RICHTER. Good. That's alright. Hemmel. Propose our toast.

HEMMEL. I drink to nothing. I salute nothing. I worship nothing. To nothing.

ALL. To nothing.

RICHTER. Only a race of genius could drink to a meta-physical entity. We are to be congratulated. We are a race of genius.

(The party is beginning to go sour. Too much drink, food, etc. is making them heavy and tired and stale. With the exception of RICHTER who remains fairly clear.)

GOMBRICH. That boy is not used to celebration. That boy is half asleep.

(HEMMEL shakes HANS roughly)

HEMMEL. Wake up, Mueller. Your eyes are closing, Mueller.

HANS. I am awake, Herr Hemmel. There is no need to shake my arm like that.

RICHTER. He is tired. Give him some more wine.

GOMBRICH. He'll be ill if he has more wine, Leader. He'll fall off his seat and crash his head on the floor.

HEMMEL. More will be a torture to him. Give him more wine, Gombrich. Let him learn the pain of being a man.

RICHTER. Drink up, Hans.

HANS. I don't think I will, Leader.

RICHTER. Drink. God damn and blast it, what are you? A puking boy. Drink. A full glass. A full red glass. Down with it. Fill his glass, Gombrich.

GOMBRICH. Here you are, Hans. Like the Leader says, a full glass.

RICHTER. You, too, Hemmel. You too, Gombrich.

GOMBRICH. My stomach is lined with lead. I can drink till my eyes swim with wine, Leader.

RICHTER. Till your senses are pickled. Good, Gombrich. What d'you say, Hemmel?

HEMMEL. I drink, Leader, until I'm wading in wine, till it

127

spurts from my toenails. I drink till it shows through my skin, till my brains splash in it.

RICHTER. More wine, then, more wine.

(They drink)

Now then, now then. I'll tell you something.

GOMBRICH. The Leader is going to tell us something.

RICHTER. I'll tell you of a dark warm night I walked in the castle garden, a moonless night, no, I lie, not moonless but heavy, dark clouds and a thin moon, a warm, close night, in the dead end of summer. I walked and met, also alone and walking, the leader.

HEMMEL. I drink to the leader.

RICHTER. Yes. Drink to him. Hello, Richter, he said. Good evening, leader, said I. You look pensive, Richter, he said. Yes, leader, I replied, I was brooding. Tell me what makes you pensive, Richter, he said. I feel sad myself. I'm not sad, leader, I answered. I am sad, Richter, he said. Look at my shadow, Richter. Why, leader? I enquired. Well, he said, answer me this question, who walks in the shadow of a leader? No-one, I retorted, except those who follow. No, said he, not all of them, Richter, only those who are close to the leader, as close as his own shadow. Ah, I said, I begin to guess your meaning. I thought you would guess it, Richter, the leader continued. Those who follow in the shadow of a leader are themselves leaders. Yes. This thought troubles me. Leader, I said, there is an old Swebish legend I remember about a warrior who brought a message of iron and blood to the people. And one day, in the dark of a garden the people came and took him, by torchlight, and led him to torture and death. I know the legend, he said. A man of blood and iron. You know, Richter, what they made of his message. No, leader, I replied. Milk and water, he said, milk and water. And he roared with laughter. Then he turned to me and said, there is another story, of a man who trod out of hell with music, with a sad song. He climbed and climbed

up from the smoke and the fires, up to a faint glimpse
of the sky. And as he reached out he turned once and
looked backwards. Yes, leader, it is a very peculiar
legend, I said. He was torn to pieces on the sea-shore
by some savage women. The strong, he said, must
never be weak. The strong are torn to pieces by the
strength of weakness.

HANS. Why do you tell this story, Leader?

GOMBRICH. You are telling us something, Leader.
Hemmel, the leader is telling us something.

HEMMEL. I am swimming in a sea of red wine, Gombrich.
A sea of red wine. The wine is choking me. I am
drowning in... a... sea of red wine.

GOMBRICH. Listen, Hemmel, don't drown. Damn and
blast you. I've seen men choked in their own blood.
I've seen men drowned in ponds of blood. I've seen the
sky all streaked with it, the ground caked with it, I've
seen so much, the food was smeared with it, hands red
with it, eyes gorged on it. Hemmel, Leader, I've
seen... so much...

(HEMMEL and GOMBRICH are sprawled on the table.
They sleep)

RICHTER. Hans. Hans. Listen. Wake up. Come here,
Hans.

HANS. (Dully) Leader?

RICHTER. Come here, Hans. Kneel down, in front of me.

HANS. Kneel, Leader?

RICHTER. Yes. Here, in front of me. Listen, Hans, what
I am about to do is a very solemn and sacred thing. Lift
up your head. Now, Hans Mueller, I take this wine and
with this wine I mark your head, so, and I say to you,
Hans Mueller, this is the vow of brotherhood and
obedience. If you break this vow, Hans Mueller, you
forfeit your life, you destroy your honour, you betray

your Leader, you spit on the brotherhood. Do you understand, Hans?

HANS. Yes, Leader. I understand.

RICHTER. It is fitting, Hans, that your loyalty should be tested. I have reason to believe, to suspect, to faintly suspect, that one of you is a traitor.

HANS. A traitor, Leader Richter. You're joking.

(He makes to rise. RICHTER holds him down by his shoulders. He stares down at him)

RICHTER. A traitor, Hans, who means to destroy the party, who means to destroy the leader. Who means to kill me. Do you know the name of that traitor, Hans? Do you know his name?

HANS. Me, Leader? No. No. I don't know...

RICHTER. God forbid that it should be you, Hans. It would be a cruel and bitter thing if it were you, Hans.

HANS. Not me, for God's sake, Leader. Not me.

RICHTER. No? No! Can I be sure? Are you the snake, the treacherous bite, the one who comes? Who knows what thoughts swirl behind your candid eyes, eh, who knows what you are plotting?

HANS. Nothing, Leader, I swear. How can I prove it?

(RICHTER comes down and kneels in front of HANS)

RICHTER. Will you prove it? Will you do it, Hans? Will you keep faith?

HANS. Yes, anything. Ask me.

RICHTER. (Whispers) One of these men is a traitor. There is a gun in the drawer of Gümmel's desk. Go and get that gun. Give me five minutes. Wait outside the door. When I call out, Hans, come in, without pause, without pause, without hesitation and when I point to the traitor, who will be revealed by then, you, Hans, you understand, without pause, without hesitation, you must kill him.

HANS. Kill him, Leader.

RICHTER. You must kill him, quick as a flash, without thought, without hesitation. Squeeze the trigger and blow off his face. Will you do this or must I doubt your loyalty? Well, Hans Mueller?

(Pause)

HANS. Yes, Leader. I will do it.

RICHTER. Good. Go then, wait for the signal and when it is given, let it be done.

HANS. Yes, Leader. (He rises, goes to the door)

RICHTER. Hans.

(HANS pauses)

Whom do you hope it will be?

HANS. It doesn't matter, Leader. I have no feelings, one way or the other. (He goes out, closing the door behind him)

(RICHTER rises. He walks round the table surveying the two drunken men. He smiles. He lifts up HEMMEL's head. HEMMEL opens his eyes. He says 'Leader'. RICHTER drops his head down again. He goes round and sits himself in his chair. He pours out a glass of wine. He raises it to each in turn)

RICHTER. I drink to animals, to the princely carnivores, lions, leopards, cheetahs, I drink to that bloodthirsty king of brutes, the master of meat, to man and his hyenas. Richter, I rise and drink. To animals. (He drinks) That's a callous boy, that. (He lifts up GOMBRICH's head) And this is a dumb, faithful, killing brute. (Drops GOMBRICH's head; lifts up

131

HEMMEL's) And you, yes, dear Hemmel, dear friend, you, I have something for you. A slow fire, a splash of acid. Hemmel. What have I got for your services?

(HEMMEL's eyes open)

HEMMEL. (Speaking distinctly) I don't understand you, Leader. I don't understand.

RICHTER. My dear Hemmel. Are you, then, so innocent. Has the wine scattered your wits. Hemmel, can I trust you?

HEMMEL. Of course, Leader, without doubt. Completely.

RICHTER. And what about him, Gombrich. Can I trust him?

HEMME. Huh. That dolt, Leader. That donkey will follow his master. Huh. Through heat, through cold. Anywhere, anytime; that dolt.

RICHTER. Gombrich would not like to hear you call him a dolt. Gombrich, you dolt, you lump, wake up, you sot. Wake up.

GOMBRICH. I am awake, Leader.

RICHTER. Are you a sot, Gombrich? Are you a dolt, my old, doltish friend?

GOMBRICH. Only you can say so, Leader.

RICHTER. Ah, but Gombrich, Hemmel says so. Don't you, Hemmel?

HEMMEL. I... a sort of a joke, Leader.

GOMBRICH. That grey rat says I am a dolt, that twisted evil rodent, that biting sewer thing; that. That!

HEMMEL. (Angrily) Yes. Dolt. Stupid. Fool. Ass. Goat. Crippled dumb monster. Fit for nothing but burdens. Arms and legs, that's what you are. Nothing.

GOMBRICH. I tell you, grey object, when I see you I smell corpses. Your face is dead, Hemmel, your fingers are dead, Hemmel. What keeps you moving, then, what's inside, some kind of slithering grey creature, something that keeps you jerking, some kind of nasty gnawing hunger. What are you, animal, rat, hyena, jackal, wolf?

HEMMEL. When I kill you, Gombrich, I will remind you slowly of all your failures, all your treacheries.

RICHTER. What's that? Gombrich a traitor?

GOMBRICH. He's a liar. He'd kill his own father for practise. He'd skin his children to keep his hand in. He's as treacherous as a...

HEMMEL. As treacherous as a... What Gombrich? Monster, renegade, coward. What, as treacherous as a...?

GOMBRICH. Hemmel!

HEMMEL. Gombrich! I'll go for your eyes, cripple.

(They grapple with each other slowly. They break apart. They circle the table. RICHTER drinks some wine. He salutes them. They are very drunk. They take up a fork each. They prowl round each other)

GOMBRICH. I'll break your back, Hemmel. I'll hear it crack. Your mother was a whore, Hemmel.

HEMMEL. Fool. Fool.

(They grapple. The door bursts open. HANS is waving a gun. He stares at them)

HANS. Hemmel, Gombrich. Listen. What are you doing? Listen. (He fires the gun) Gümmel is alive. He's not dead. Richter lied to us. Gümmel is alive.

(They all turn and face RICHTER. RICHTER rises)

GOMBRICH. What does this mean, Leader?

HEMMEL. Idiot. Nincompoop. It's obvious. It means Gümmel's alive. It means, Richter lied to us.

RICHTER. I lied to you, Gombrich. Hemmel is right.

HEMMEL. What are you doing with that pistol, Hans?

HANS. He told me to get it. He said go and get a gun and the one I point to you have to shoot. He said he'd be a traitor.

GOMBRICH. The Leader said that?

HEMMEL. Of course he did. Can't your brain grasp it, Gombrich? He set us at each other's throats and the one that's left goes bang.

GOMBRICH. But why, Hemmel? Why should the Leader do that?

HEMMEL. That, Gombrich, is an excellent question, a beautiful question. I admire you, Gombrich, for the way you put that question. It is a question to which I long to hear the answer. To find that answer I intend to apply myself to Leader Richter. After a time, no doubt there will be an answer.

RICHTER. I will tell you now, animals. It is very simple. I have an interest in your deaths. It would be a sunny and pleasant time for me when you are dead, you, Mueller, you Gombrich, you, yes, you, Hemmel. I had a deep desire for your deaths. I thought it fitting that a Swebish man should enjoy the fact of your deaths.

GOMBRICH. Swebish. Who is Swebish? Richter? Who is Swebish?

HEMMEL. That man, that man there, that slow, fat man. Leader Richter. Now I recognise it clearly. I smell it. He gives off the sweet smell, the fetid odour of a Swebisher. Can you smell it, Hans? Is your nose trained like mine?

HANS. I notice the face, Herr Hemmel. That is enough.

GOMBRICH. By God. You are right, Hemmel. It is written all over him. What a dishonour for us. I feel degraded.

HEMMEL. Richter. We have something to do, Herr Richter. Gentlemen, we have something to do.

(They move towards RICHTER)

HANS. Shall I shoot him, Herr Hemmel?

HEMMEL. Not yet. Not yet.

SCENE FIVE

(Scene in the garden. Darkness. Song 'Im Wald Und Auf Der Heide'. While the song is playing, lanterns cross and recross the stage.

GOMBRICH comes in, raises his lantern. Goes hurrying off. Enter HANS from the other side, peers round, goes off. Enter HEMMEL from other side, passes HANS, peers around him. He is shadowed by RICHTER, without lantern. HEMMEL stops, turns round, so does RICHTER. HEMMEL hurries off. Enter GOMBRICH, HANS, they pass one another. There is a crash, a cry. Voices, very drunk, are heard. Enter HEMMEL, crawling. Shadowed by RICHTER. GOMBRICH calls, off)

GOMBRICH. Hemmel. Is that you?

HEMMEL. (Appears with lantern, crawling) Gombrich, you drunken swine. I'm hurt. Where are you?

GOMBRICH. Hemmel. Here, Hemmel. Hurry, man. I think I see him.

HEMMEL. My leg's broken. Give me some help.

GOMBRICH. Hurry, Hemmel. Hurry, you fool.

HANS. (Off) Herr Gombrich, where are you? Ah.

HEMMEL. Have you got him, Mueller? Have you got the swine?

HANS. Help, Gombrich, Hemmel. He's squeezing me to

136

death. He's like a gorilla.

GOMBRICH. Is it you, Mueller? Is it you, you stupid boy?

HANS. Are you blind, old man? Do I look like a Swebisher?

HEMMEL. My leg is broken. Mueller. Gombrich. If he finds me he'll kill me. He'll kill a helpless man. He's a wild beast. (He sees RICHTER) Let me alone, Richter. Richter, I appeal to you. It's all a mistake. Let me go, Richter. I forgive you, I promise.

GOMBRICH. Hemmel, I can't find you.

HEMMEL. Here, here. He's here, Gombrich.

RICHTER. Is it you, Hemmel? Is it you? Are you hurt, then, my poor fellow?

HEMMEL. They're all mad, Leader. It was all their idea, Richter. It was a test, you see. I understand that now. You were testing us. Help me into the house and we'll barricade the door against those wild animals.

RICHTER. You were hunting me, Hemmel. You were after my blood.

GOMBRICH. Is that you, Hemmel?

(HEMMEL catches hold of RICHTER)

HEMMEL. The swine is here, Gombrich. I've got him, I've got him. Quick. He's murdering me.

HANS. I can see you, Herr Hemmel. I'm coming.

(RICHTER struggles free)

HEMMEL. He's getting away. Quick, my boy. Hurry.

(Enter HANS)

HANS. Where did he go?

HEMMEL. That way. Never mind that. I'm in terrible pain.

HANS. My poor Hemmel. Let me see. Does it hurt, my poor friend?

HEMMEL. Of course it hurts. My leg is broken.

HANS. Let me see.

HEMMEL. Don't touch me. Don't... ah.

(HANS fingers the leg)

HANS. It's not broken.

HEMMEL. You're a stupid boy. I can feel the bone grating. What are you doing?

HANS. It's not broken, Herr Hemmel. I tell you. There. Try to walk.

HEMMEL. I can't... (He staggers to his feet) You are right! It's only severely bruised. Thank God for that. I thought it was broken. The pain was considerable.

GOMBRICH. (Off) Ah. (Pause) Welcome, Leader Richter. Welcome.

(Pause)

HEMMEL. The pain is very great, Mueller. I need assistance. Help me to the house. Bring the traitor, Gombrich, you bear. Keep him tight.

(GOMBRICH appears with RICHTER)

GOMBRICH. I hold him tight, Hemmel. He will not run away.

HEMMEL. He is strangely quiet. Help me, Mueller. The pain is very great but I am happy.

(MARIE calls)

138

MARIE. Hans, where are you?

HANS. Here, Marie. We have captured Richter. Poor
Hemmel is hurt. But Gombrich and I are safe and well.

(MARIE appears)

MARIE. What are you doing to Herr Richter?

HEMMEL. We are to consider the question of the man
Richter and to reason with him, Marie. That is all.

HANS. Go in, Marie. This is official business.

GOMBRICH. Come along. I'm very sleepy. At my age I
need a good night's rest.

HEMMEL. Herr Richter also is tired. Soon he will sleep
like a child, like a little child.

(Song 'Gute Nacht'. They take RICHTER away)

SCENE SIX

(As in Scene One. The room in darkness. The door
opens. Enter HEMMEL. He calls)

HEMMEL. We'll bring the Swebisher in here, Gombrich.

GOMBRICH. (Off) You keep your orders to yourself,
Hemmel. I don't take orders from the likes of you.

HEMMEL. Don't be so sensitive. This is a civilian matter,
Gombrich. In civilian matters the responsibility is
mine.

GOMBRICH. As long as we understand each other, Hemmel.

(Enter HANS)

HANS. Shall we use the cage, Herr Hemmel?

HEMMEL. Of course not, Mueller. That was a typical
Swebisher trick. We do not act in that manner. We are
more civilized, more humane.

GOMBRICH. Shall I bring him in now?

HEMMEL. One moment. Hans, where is Gümmel?

HANS. He's locked in a room upstairs, Hemmel. I heard
him moving about when I went for the gun, you see. He
shouted 'Is that you, Richter?' That's when I knew what
was going on.

HEMMEL. Clever, Mueller. You have a future. Gümmel
is a problem, I see that. We can either release him

and say that Richter was mad...

HANS. But...

HEMMEL. Or we can release Gümmel from his physical body to join this other Swebisher in their Swebisher sky and say they killed each other.

HANS. Ah!

HEMMEL. Of the two...

(The light clicks on. GÜMMEL is revealed, seated at his desk. He smiles)

GÜMMEL. Well, Hemmel, 'of the two', you were saying?

HEMMEL. What's this? Another of those Swebish... pardon me, Herr Gümmel. You took me by surprise. I am glad to see you safe and sound. When that madman Richter told us you were dead I knew all our lives were in danger. What mad scheme he had in mind...

GÜMMEL. Gombrich.

GOMBRICH. (Off) Who is that, you, Hans? Up to your tricks again.

GÜMMEL. Come in, Gombrich. Bring Herr Richter with you.

GOMBRICH. Oh, God. Is that you, Herr Gümmel? At once, Herr Gümmel. Come along, pig. Don't you hear Herr Gümmel...?

GÜMMEL. Gently Gombrich. You are a rough fellow. Surely you don't wish to harm Herr Richter?

(GOMBRICH enters with RICHTER)

GOMBRICH. Here he is, Herr Gümmel. This is a surprise indeed, Herr Gümmel. A good surprise for us, eh, Hemmel? Eh, Mueller?

141

GÜMMEL. Good evening, Martin. I hope you are well.

(Pause)

You are not usually so backward in coming forward,
Martin. What have you to say for yourself, eh?

(Pause)

RICHTER. Least said, soonest mended, Herr Gümmel.

GÜMMEL. I see. I see. You Gombrich, what have you got
to say for yourself.

GOMBRICH. I'm too old, Herr Gümmel. I'm easily
confused. First you give orders, then Richter, then
Hemmel. The command structure is very confusing.
What am I to do? Who is the leader here, Herr
Gümmel?

GÜMMEL. Ah, that's it. When the command structure is
confused what is a man's duty? Who's to say? I
sympathise, Gombrich.

GOMBRICH. Am I to take it that you are in command, then,
Herr Gümmel?

GÜMMEL. It appears to be so, Gombrich.

GOMBRICH. I'm very glad that is cleared up, Herr
Gümmel. That puts everything in order. What are your
orders, Herr Gümmel?

GÜMMEL. Well, if I am in command what would you
suggest by way of punishment for such monstruous
insubordination.

GOMBRICH. Well, Herr Gümmel, that is not for me to say.
If I were to suggest anything it would be that the worst
offender should be flogged and then shot, the least
offender should be spared the unmilitary degradation
of flogging.

GÜMMEL. Spoken like a man. Well, now, what would you

142

suggest, Hans?

HANS. Me, Herr Gümmel?

GÜMMEL. You, Hans.

HANS. We were led astray, Herr Gümmel. I liked none of
it. First Herr Richter, then Herr Hemmel, and Herr
Gombrich. I am young, Herr Gümmel, inexperienced.
I look for guidance from my elders and betters. When
they let me down it's not surprising I go to the dogs.

GÜMMEL. Of course, of course. What, then, do you
suggest as a punishment?

HANS. Well, the authorities are the right persons to deal
with this. That's my opinion, Herr Gümmel, for what
it's worth. The authorities know what to do. They have
the law and punishment and I'm sure if you handed the
criminals over to them justice would be done.

GÜMMEL. And what about yourself, Hans. What punishment
would you suggest for yourself?

HANS. I think a case can be made out for leniency, there,
Herr Gümmel. As I say, I'm young, inexperienced. I
haven't yet learned to recognise true authority when I
see it. I laugh when I think how I took these creatures
for authorities when now I can see quite clearly that you
are the one to be obeyed. That is quite clear to me now.

GÜMMEL. Well argued, Mueller. Anything else?

HANS. I would remind Herr Gümmel of the fact that I am
an expectant father and that is a great responsibility.
Marie is a good girl but she cannot be expected to know
what is best, being a woman, that is.

GÜMMEL. Indeed. I am very grateful to Marie, Hans. It
was she who had the kindness to let me out when you
were all hooting and shouting in the garden.

HANS. I'm glad of that, Herr Gümmel. She has good
instincts and no doubt she will make a good mother of

our child.

GÜMMEL. Well, there it is, then. Leniency for you and the police and prison for the rest.

HEMMEL. One moment, Herr Gümmel. You have not asked my opinion yet. I am a human being. Sick and in pain as I am, I demand a hearing.

GÜMMEL. Demand, Hemmel?

HEMMEL. Pardon, Herr Gümmel. My expression was rather unfortunate. Shall I say... ?

GÜMMEL. Say no more, Hemmel. It will be interesting to hear your views on the topic.

HEMMEL. My views are simple, Herr Gümmel. I am a loyal son of the National Health Party. What I have done I have done for the party. Some day, if not today then the next, or the next, the party will rise and when it does it will rise on the arms of those who have been strong in the dark hours.

GÜMMEL. Are you asking for a medal, Hemmel?

HEMMEL. No, Herr Gümmel. What I am saying is this, it would be most unfortunate for us if we were to be imprisoned and it would be most unfortunate for you if it were ever known that you helped us to conceal ourselves, and very unfortunate for you if it were ever known in certain circles that you harboured a Swebisher in your house, even in the time of battle.

GÜMMEL. What should I do, then, Hemmel?

HEMMEL. Let us go, Herr Gümmel. It is as simple as that, let us go.

GÜMMEL. Thank you, Hemmel. You have been clear and helpful. If Herr Richter would condescend to speak I should know how we stand. Richter, will you not speak to us? Richter, Richter, Richter. Tell us what to do?

(Pause)

GÜMMEL. No. Nothing. Nothing at all. Perhaps you
saved my life, Martin. Perhaps these gentlemen would
have seen me off if you hadn't managed things.

GOMBRICH. Never, Herr Gümmel. Simply following
orders.

HEMMEL. It was not our intention, Herr Gümmel.

HANS. What Herr Hemmel says is quite correct. We were
carried away by the force and power of Herr Richter's
rhetoric. We were misled.

GÜMMEL. Carried away by the force of your rhetoric,
Martin. And now not a word. Is your mouth dry, then.
Is your tongue dead.

RICHTER. The fires have all gone out, Herr Gümmel. The
smoke is in my mouth.

GÜMMEL. What, is that all? That is nothing whatever to
say. You must do better than that.

RICHTER. I would like...

GÜMMEL. Yes?

RICHTER. I would like... words roll dead off my tongue.
If my breath were a gale... my voice... a clap of
thunder... they would be too heavy.

HEMMEL. He's drunk, Herr Gümmel. He's a drunken
madman.

GÜMMEL. Is that it? Are you drunk, Martin?

RICHTER. I would like to... say... goodbye... to all the
faces that walked past me in my nightmare, goodbye
friends, goodbye Helmut, Johan, Georg, Ute, Gerda,
Anna, too many names to say goodbye to, too many
faces that mourn past my eyes with their long dead
lives wrapped round them... smoke has made my eyes

145

all red... I can't see... Helmut, Anna... smoke in
the sky... smoke in my mouth... in my mouth... the
taste of smoke... in my mouth. Herr Gümmel... I
see backwards... whenever I look... I see backwards.

GÜMMEL. What nonsense it all is. What a crafty fellow you
are, Martin, pretending to be drunk. You are no help at
all.

GOMBRICH. He's insane. Helmut, Johan, Inge... who are
those people, Hemmel?

HEMMEL. It's a pack of lies. There are no such people.

GÜMMEL. I must say, gentlemen, you're not much help
either. Whenever I stop speaking you fall to quarrelling.
Except Martin here, who pretends to be drunk or mad.
Gentlemen, this is all fantasy. All dreams. Let me ask
you a question. Now listen carefully... you too, Herr
Richter... and give me your answer.

GOMBRICH, HEMMEL and HANS. Yes, Herr Gümmel.

GÜMMEL. Well, now, tell me, before the National Health
Party, before the Free Action Party, before this party
and that party, where gentlemen, where, in the whole
world, was I? Answer me that. Gombrich?

GOMBRICH. You, Herr Gümmel?

GÜMMEL. Me, Herr Gombrich.

GOMBRICH. You... you were here, Herr Gümmel.

GÜMMEL. In this beautiful house, Gombrich, in these
large grounds, Gombrich, in this beautiful mansion
with its multiplicity of facilities... you are saying that's
where I was?

GOMBRICH. Certainly. That is so, is it now, Herr Gümmel?

GÜMMEL. Perfectly correct, Gombrich. That is where I
was. And Mueller, in the days of conflict, in the days
of greatness and battle and death and defeat, where was

146

I then, do you think? Can you answer that question?

HANS. To the best of my knowledge and belief, Herr Gümmel, you were here, in this house.

GÜMMEL. Here and elsewhere. In this house, young man, with its gardens, plantations, its tall windows, its fine chimneys, its big fires, its many rooms, here and elsewhere, Mueller.

HANS. I believe so, Herr Gümmel.

GÜMMEL. And Hemmel, after the slaughter, after all the buildings were gutted, after the fire raids, the shells, the many lives gone, after the torture and slow death of the people, the death of the party, what become of me. Where was I to be found?

HEMMEL. Why here, of course, Herr Gümmel. Where else?

GÜMMEL. Why here, of course. In my splendid residence, with its trees, orchards, flowers in profusion. Here and elsewhere, in my vineyards, my factories, my plantations, my farms, walking here and walking there, business, business, business. Here I was, there I was, and here I am and continue to be. It is a fine story. Martin, Martin, answer. When everything was dying did I not flourish, did I not expand, did I not grow and thrive. Answer.

RICHTER. So you did. So you did. Unforgivable.

GÜMMEL. What has forgiveness to do with it? I was, I am, I will be. Indestructable, necessary, purveyor and conveyor of old truths. Is that not so?

HANS. I am amazed, Herr Gümmel. Your case is so persuasive.

GÜMMEL. You are young, Hans, you see clearly. These old ones are blind with legends and mysteries. Shall I tell you the great meaning of my life? Are you too old to learn it?

HEMMEL. We are never too old to learn, Herr Gümmel.

GÜMMEL. Good, good. The first truth is this. A good
day's work for a good day's pay. Now, isn't that
impressive. Please, for my sake, repeat after me.
A good day's work for a good day's pay.

ALL. A good day's...

(GÜMMEL prompts them)

GÜMMEL. ... work...

ALL. ... work... for a good day's pay.

GÜMMEL. Good fellows. Splendid. And now for the second
truth... honesty is the best policy.

ALL. Honesty is...

GÜMMEL. the best policy.

ALL. the best policy.

GÜMMEL. Excellent. And now a great truth. A beautiful,
marvellous, wonderful truth. Listen, all of you. To
him that has, more shall be given, to him that hasn't,
even what he has shall be stripped from him. Can you
remember that. To him that has...

ALL. To him that has...

GÜMMEL. Shall be given...

ALL. Shall be given.

GÜMMEL. To him that has not...

ALL. To him that has not...

GÜMMEL. Even that which he has...

ALL. Even that which he has...

GÜMMEL. Even that, even that SHALL BE TAKEN AWAY.

ALL. Even that, even that, shall be taken away.

GÜMMEL. There, that is it. Now you know. There need
be no more strife. There is work, there is joy for all.
Things pile on things. The earth will groan to the
power of our labour, the earth will teem. On a mountain
of goods higher, higher, higher we rise, each grows on
his own mountain, some small, some great. And the
greatest of all is Gümmel.

ALL. The greatest of all is Gümmel.

GÜMMEL. Yes, yes. This is wonderful. This is grand.
Forget old strifes. Hans will marry Marie and a young
worker will be born. There is a place prepared for him.
I can promise him that. Marie. Marie. Come along.

MARIE. Herr Gümmel.

GÜMMEL. Bless you, my child. Go to your husband. Take
her by the hand, Hans. Gombrich, Hemmel, Richter,
forget old wounds, old strife. Live in the eternity of my
pleasure. There is work for all. Keep the house clean,
the fires burning, the chimneys swept. Look to the
washing machines, the spin driers, the oil-fired
heaters, the limousines, the refrigerators, look to the
lathes, the rachettes, the cranes, tractors, keep it
going, keep it going. Gümmel's appetite is insatiable.
Isms are nothing, divisions are nothing, hate each
other, love each other, what does Gümmel care about
that, he is good, wise, generous, indestructable.
Gümmel the creator, Gümmel the financier, Gümmel
the be all and end all. That is my name. The three
names of Gümmel.

HANS. Oh, it's marvellous. Why did nobody ever tell me?

MARIE. Herr Gümmel is not one to take people into his
confidence unless he trusts them, Hans.

GÜMMEL. Well said, Marie. I trust you, friends. Forget
old ties, old scars, let the dead fuss over the dead.

149

Let them rot in peace. Ours is the glory, the great
material glory of production. Not an hour, a minute, a
second, must be wasted. It is all too precious. I am
hungry and famished. I need, you need. Let us act
together. Our interests are identical. Your work, my
endeavour, your hands, my brain.

ALL. Gümmel, Gümmel.

GÜMMEL. I see a new future for you all. For me nothing
ever changes. But I see for you a new and practical
future, without remorse, without sin. Each man his
own form of transportation, each man his own four
bedroomed, detached residence. Well, Martin. What
do you say?

(RICHTER draws out his white butler's gloves, slowly
draws them on)

RICHTER. Will you be dressing for dinner, Herr Gümmel?

GÜMMEL. As usual, Richter. I shall be entertaining a
small party. You will see to it.

RICHTER. Certainly, Herr Gümmel.

GÜMMEL. I'm glad we've had this talk. There's been some
slackness lately. I know you have private problems, but
private difficulties must not be allowed to impede the
smooth running of the economy. Gombrich, I notice a
deterioration in the front gardens. Those lawns... need
I say more?

GOMBRICH. I will see to it, Herr Gümmel. I ask your
pardon.

GÜMMEL. Off you go then. Tomorrow I will examine the
grounds.

GOMBRICH. At once, Herr Gümmel. Herr Richter, will
you be needing me for house duty?

RICHTER. I think not, Gombrich. Herr Gümmel is not
expecting a large gathering.

GOMBRICH. Thank you, Herr Richter. Herr Gümmel.

(He clicks his heels and leaves)

GÜMMEL. Hemmel, the heating arrangements, they are far from satisfactory.

HEMMEL. It's the main thermostat, Herr Gümmel. But I think I can fix it until we get a replacement.

GÜMMEL. See to it, then.

HEMMEL. Will I be expected to wait at table, Herr Richter?

RICHTER. I will decide about that later, Hemmel.

HEMMEL. Of course, Herr Richter. Of course.

(He bows and departs)

GÜMMEL. Hans?

HANS. Herr Gümmel?

GÜMMEL. I shall be working late after my guests have gone, on the power point project. You will see that all the relevant papers are ready for me?

HANS. Certainly, Herr Gümmel. The project has reached an interesting phase.

GÜMMEL. Fascinating. Fascinating.

(HANS bows and leaves)

MARIE. Shall I tidy up here, Herr Gümmel?

GÜMMEL. Later, Marie. Later. For now I think you had better begin to prepare the dining-room. My guests are important. They'll expect nothing but perfection.

MARIE. Thank you, Herr Gümmel. I aim to give satisfaction.

GÜMMEL. Off you go, then.

RICHTER. I will go and lay out your things, Herr Gümmel.

GÜMMEL. My portrait, Richter. It seems to have got it-self moved somewhere. Find it, will you.

RICHTER. Your portrait. Good gracious. So it does. Ah! Here it is, Herr Gümmel. The cord seems to have broken. I'll see to it at once.

GÜMMEL. Good. See to it. And when you have seen to it, see that my bath is ready, will you, Martin?

(He rises and goes out. RICHTER bows. RICHTER stands with the portrait. He lifts it up, looks at it. Puts it down. Stands. Calls.)

RICHTER. Helmut. Anna. Johann, Johann, Johann.

GÜMMEL. (Off) Richter. My bath. I'm waiting.

RICHTER. Coming, Herr Gümmel.

(He puts his hands to his cheeks. To his head. He straightens his jacket. Corrects his tie. He takes out a comb and combs his hair)

Coming... Herr Gümmel.

(He leaves. The stage is silent. MARIE and HANS return. They bow to the audience. HEMMEL and GOMBRICH come in. They also bow. Then GUMMEL and RICHTER. GUMMEL takes his portrait and stands behind it)

GÜMMEL. All friends. Feuds forgotten.

RICHTER. How nice everything is.

HEMMEL. Shall we sing the evening song, Herr Gümmel?

GÜMMEL. What a good idea. Hemmel, will you give us a chord.

152

(HEMMEL takes out a tuning fork and sounds it. They all test their voices. HEMMEL steps forward and conducts.)

HEMMEL. One, two, three...

(Song: 'GUTEN ABEND, GUT' NACHT'. They bow, smile, clap. Bow again. Go off. CURTAIN closes on song: 'ES KLAPPERT DIE MUHLE'.

OTHER C AND B PLAYSCRIPTS

* PS 1	TOM PAINE Paul Foster	*21s +6s6d
* PS 2	BALLS and other plays (The Recluse, Hurrah for the Bridge, The Hessian Corporal) Paul Foster	*25s +7s6d
PS 3	THREE PLAYS (Lunchtime Concert, Coda, The Inhabitants) Olwen Wymark	*21s +6s6d
* PS 4	CLEARWAY Vivienne C. Welburn	*21s +6s6d
* PS 5	JOHNNY SO LONG and THE DRAG Vivienne C. Welburn	*25s +9s0d
* PS 6	SAINT HONEY and OH DAVID, ARE YOU THERE? Paul Ritchie	*25s +10s6d
PS 7	WHY BOURNEMOUTH? and other plays (An Apple a Day, The Missing Links) John Antrobus	*25s +9s0d
* PS 8	THE CARD INDEX and other plays (The Interrupted Act, Gone Out) Tadeusz Rosewicz trans. Adam Czerniawski	*25s +10s6d
PS 9	US Peter Brook and others	*42s +21s
* PS 10	SILENCE and THE LIE Nathalie Sarraute trans. Maria Jolas	*25s + 9s0d

PS 23   SPRING AWAKENING
        Frank Wedekind
        Trans. Tom Osborn   *25s +9s0d

PS 24   PRECIOUS MOMENTS FROM THE
        FAMILY ALBUM TO PROVIDE YOU
        WITH COMFORT IN THE LONG YEARS
        TO COME
        Naftali Yavin   *25 +9s0d

* PS 25 DESIRE CAUGHT BY THE TAIL
        Pablo Picasso
        trans. Roland Penrose   *18s +7s6d

* PS 26 THE BREASTS OF TIRESIAS
        Guillaume Apollinaire
        trans. A.M. Sheridan Smith   *18s +7s6d

* PS 27 ANNA-LUSE and other plays
        David Mowat   *30s +12s0d

* PS 28 O and other plays
        Sandro Key-Aaberg   *25s +9s0d

* PS 29 WELCOME TO DALLAS, MR KENNEDY
        Kaj Himmelstrup   *25s +9s0d

PS 30   THE LUNATIC, THE SECRET SPORTSMAN
        AND THE WOMEN NEXT DOOR and other
        plays
        Stanley Eveling   *25s +8s6d

* PS 31 STRINDBERG
        Colin Wilson   *25s +9s0d.

* PS 32 THE FOUR LITTLE GIRLS
        Pablo Picasso
        trans. Roland Penrose   *25s +9s0d

                    * Hardcover + Paperback

* Plays marked thus are represented for dramatic present-
ation by C and B (Theatre) Ltd, 18 Brewer Street, London W1